CHAKRA WORKOUT

Blawyn and Jones

PUSTAK MAHAL®
DELHI • MUMBAI • PATNA • BANGALORE • HYDERABAD

Copyright © in India by
Pustak Mahal®, Delhi

J-3/16 , Daryaganj, New Delhi-110002
☎ 23276539, 23272783, 23272784 • *Fax:* 011-23260518
E-mail: info@pustakmahal.com • *Website:* www.pustakmahal.com

Sales Centres
10-B, Netaji Subhash Marg, Daryaganj, New Delhi-110002
☎ 23268292, 23268293, 23279900 • *Fax:* 011-23280567
E-mail: rapidexdelhi@indiatimes.com

Branch Offices
Bangalore: ☎ 22234025
E-mail: pmblr@sancharnet.in • pustak@sancharnet.in
Mumbai: ☎ 22010941
E-mail: rapidex@bom5.vsnl.net.in
Patna: ☎ 3094193 • *Telefax:* 0612-2322719
E-mail: rapidexptn@rediffmail.com
Hyderabad: *Telefax:* 040-24737290
E-mail: pustakmahalhyd@yahoo.co.in

Reprinted from:
'CHAKRA WORKOUT for Body, Mind & Spirit'
© 1997, Blwyn and Jones

Published by:
Llewellyn Publications
St. Paul, MN 55 164, USA

ISBN 81-223-0062-6

Contents

PREFACE

This book will start the process of directing your energy into your higher chakras and making the lower chakras healthy enough to stand the increased "voltage."

Normally, without direction, your lower chakras are more dense, "heavier," and have a slower vibrational rate. Conversely, the farther away a chakra is from your base, the higher its frequency and the less dense it is.

For us, alchemy is the process of transforming and transmuting lower chakra energies into "higher," more refined frequencies. This is looking at the alchemy of spiritual transformation from a Tantric viewpoint. The essence of the process is not to reject the lower energies, but to consciously transmute those energies in your alchemy of personal spiritual transformation.

If our words help you in any way in your spiritual quest, then we will feel our endeavor has been successful.

INTRODUCTION

Sitting for years on a Himalayan mountaintop is a valid way to achieve spiritual progress, but the average Westerner has neither the time nor the patience to do this. In the West, life is fast-paced and the hours and strength we have to devote to spiritual or physical practices are limited. We need to achieve definite results quickly, because most of us can set aside only a few minutes each day for whatever technique we have chosen.

There are many paths to spiritual awareness. This book is not trying to present the "truth," because our truths may never be yours. Always be aware of what realities are valid for you, and be alert to changes in your perceptions as you grow spiritually. It is you, the individual, who must develop awareness of what is working for you and what is not. Don't ever complacently decide, "This is truth." A pond stagnates when there is no influx of fresh water, no mixing of old and new, no movement onward. So the constant flow of your seeking, expanding, and growing will keep your "truth" alive and ever-changing.

Since we are presently in physical bodies, why not start a spiritual quest with the physical body itself, since that is what we are more closely in touch with? Therefore, this is a beginner's guide on movement and breath. Imagine it as a signpost at a crossroads saying, "Self-discovery begins here."

Certain physical movements combined with consciously controlled breath can acquaint you with your energy body. Cosmic energy is all around us — we are cosmic energy. Our spiritual progress begins as we learn to generate, cultivate, and move energy within ourselves. Dynamic meditation has been very helpful and we would like to share these exercises and meditation combinations with others who are also searching.

Truth

Are you sure you are right?
Quite, quite sure?
Being "right" closes doors
On other people's "rights"
Who think you are wrong,
Even as you believe they
Are wrong.
There's never just one right.
There are as many rights
As there are people,
And just as many wrongs.
Keep the doors of your mind open
So the rights and wrongs and in-betweens
Can pass through freely.
Among such flotsam and jetsam
Of knowledge and beliefs
Can be found a precious gem
Beyond all rights and wrongs
The center of cosmic truth.

The Aquarian Age Brings Change

In the past, usually one surrendered totally to a master. This made spiritual life much simpler, because the burden of decision was lifted from the individual. A student needed only to follow the master's instructions. These might be difficult instructions, they might have even seemed impossible, but the requirements were definite and the path to spiritual growth was well-marked.

Now, as the Age of Aquarius dawns, these traditions are losing their appeal. This is especially true in the West, where we ask questions and do not blindly accept. More and more of us are willing to venture into the unknown, to search for greater spirituality, on our own. Also, there seem to be fewer masters taking disciples; even if you desired to be a disciple, you might not be able to find a master to follow or one to whom you could surrender.

Maybe this change is due, in part, to the availability of many of the old "secrets." Guarded for so long, meted out so carefully to disciples, many of these secrets are coming out from China, Tibet, Japan, the Middle East, and from Native Americans here in North America. Many books of these secrets are now available in almost any bookstore. The oral tradition is alive and well, too, as we have learned from traveling companions and chance encounters throughout our travels.

Techniques Which Open the Door to Meditation

In a broad sense, we feel there are two types of meditation: passive and dynamic. Both are important. Many people in the West can best achieve spiritual growth through a combination of the two. There are many types of passive meditation. They are usually quiet, involving little external physical activity. More advanced techniques require much internal activity and careful circulation of the breath. There are probably as many forms of quiet, passive meditation as there are people. To find a personal, serene, unchanging center, it makes sense that each person will approach meditation from a slightly different angle.

Dynamic meditation, which is newer to some people, is movement combined with consciously directed breath. Several dynamic meditations have evolved from martial art forms. Others seem to have had their beginnings in rejuvenation techniques. In the beginning, these meditations are different from passive meditation, though the ultimate goal is the same.

When first practicing dynamic meditation, the mind is cluttered with concerns about whether the breath and the movements are synchronized correctly. It is hard to remember everything at once. This passes with practice, as each person discovers the natural way that breathing becomes a part of the movement, and begins to see the joy of dynamic meditation. This is the start of an adventure into the inner, vibrant energy space.

The movement of dynamic meditation seems especially suited to stressed Westerners. Often it is easier to relax into a truly passive meditation after dynamic moving meditation, even if a quiet mental state seemed impossible at the outset.

A Combination of Traditions

We are presenting movement systems from several traditions. T'ai Chi Chi Kung, T'ai Chi Ruler, and Red Dragon Chi Kung are Chinese. The Chakra Energizers are East Indian; Sufi Earth Dancing, Veil Dancing, and Whirling come from the Middle East. The Dance of the Four Directions is Native American.

From a strictly physical point of view, the result of movement and breath exercises can be a trimmer, more supple, healthier body that moves with increased strength and grace. Exercise of almost any kind is an uncomplicated way to feel better and look better, but these exercise meditations promise much more.

For example, the Red Dragon Chi Kung movements, which use a long wooden wand for all positions, are incredible. When combined with conscious breath, the movements generate chi quickly. The wand acts as a conductor of energy between the energy centers of the hands, the solar plexus, and the brow.

One student who took the Red Dragon Chi Kung class for eight weeks got rid of her headaches and improved her flexibility tremendously. Because of arthritis in her hands and hips, at first she couldn't do many of the positions correctly. But she continued to do them every day, and in no time was bending and stretching with the rest of the class. "I couldn't even lay my hands out flat when I started," she said, beaming, as she spread her hands straight, each joint fully extended. She had also lost 15 pounds by the end of the course.

On a spiritual level, the results can be much more dramatic as you become acquainted with the energy source that is all around and within you. We are luminous energy beings. Kirlian photography has provided tangible proof of this energy field, or aura, as it extends out from our bodies, as have other scientific machines and techniques.

Choices

How and to whom you surrender yourself is beyond the scope of this book. Whether you surrender to a bodhi leaf like the Buddha did, or to a master, or to your own inner cosmic center — it is you who makes the choices. You have to be the one who prepares your body and mind for the increasing flow of energy.

Because our bodies are our single most precious personal possession, the quality of our life, both spiritually and physically, is directly governed by our physical condition. As body tone improves, for example, mental outlook changes in many ways. New thoughts and new ideas become possible. Similar to the concept of the whole being greater than the sum of its parts, breath and movement when combined have an alchemy out of which something new and unexpected is born: an actual awareness of energy and often a new perception of spirituality.

Especially for the beginner, movement and breath become a starting point on the threshold of the doorway to spirituality. Once you can consciously feel the life force flowing through your body, and grasp the possibilities of a more spiritual life, you have taken the first step on a path of greater spiritual awareness, and possibly a step towards enlightenment.

Surrender

Surrender is tough.
Surrender is jumping
Into freefall without worry.
Surrender is losing yourself.
Surrender to someone,
Surrender to anything,
Until surrender is complete.
And you make the amazing discovery
That after all, you have
Not lost yourself.
That after all, something was
Dissolved and it was your fear.
That something was found
And it was You.

Part One

THE ELEMENTS

Here are the simplest and most traditional elements that are used to describe and work with spirituality. They all deal with the recognition, stimulation, and transmutation of the cosmic life force, which we call chi. These elements are only symbolic avenues that hopefully will aid the imagination so that you may begin to see the possibilities of the indescribable. Using these terms is the only way we know to work with such concepts.

By breaking the elements into separate sections, we are not implying any actual division. On the contrary, spirituality is one continuous, seamless reality, where each element overlaps the other. These elements do not stand on their own. The most important concept of all, we believe, is that of wholeness, the unity of everyone and everything, with no divisions or separations: the "universe," which means to become or turn toward one.

These elements, when combined with the movement exercises in Part Two, are humanity's heritage from centuries of study by the followers of many faiths and philosophies: Hinduism, Buddhism, Islam, and their derivatives; philosophies from Tibet, from the Middle East, and from Native Americans. We throw them all in the pot and a magical alchemy results. Mix them in good health.

Chi Energy

Chi is energy coursing through your body. In fact, it *is* your body. You bring it in and out when you breathe, when you eat, when you dream, whether you are asleep or awake. Without it, the physical body could not exist. When chi is recognized, nurtured, and allowed to flow freely through the body, spiritual possibilities are realized.

Do you know someone who is described as having a lot of personal magnetism? Although our understanding is imperfect, we think this quality often reflects a strong life force, and is a desired goal. Also, hormone production, the lack of it, or the misinterpretation of hormonal messages as we age appears to be a part of the formula for whether chi is strong or weak.

This flow of energy known as chi is a continuous process which gives vitality to the body. It is restricted by an overfed, inactive, inflexible body; weak or sick organs are a symptom of impaired flow. This is an imbalance that can lead to bad health. Many of us barely exist, operating on a minimum of life force. And as we grow older, the life force dwindles until we die.

Chi Is Cosmic Energy

What is this life force of the cosmos? We can only try to imagine the unimaginable. We think it is an invisible energy that makes everything possible. Humanity has tried to get at its essence through many different terms and phrases: God force, the life force, prana, a kind of primordial glue, the personal energy known as chi (sometimes written as qi or ki); for some, it might be the basis of electromagnetic energy.

All life taps into cosmic energy. Most organisms seem to naturally do a better job with this energy than humanity does. Look at the plant that performs daily magic from the raw elements of dirt, water, and sunlight. How inefficient we are in comparison! The ant, without benefit of steroids or weight training or high-tech machinery, casually carries an object, many times bigger and heavier than itself, up a vertical rock surface. How does he do it? Is he tapping into chi in a way we can only dream of?

Humanity has become too smart. We invented the wheel, became immersed in technology, and began the slow, steady "progress" of disassociating ourselves from the forces of the cosmos. We have gained Logic and lost Art. We think that Western science can only go so far — in our opinion, it has merit, but should not be a roadblock to understanding the universe.

A Universal Quest

It is certainly true that many generations of human beings in the past and up to modern times have lived with no knowledge of cosmic energy. But all through recorded history, this has indeed been a universal concept, one that has intrigued human beings for thousands of years.

What do you think of when you hear the word "alchemy"? Hocus-pocus? Laughable attempts to change lead to gold? The transmutation of lead into gold always sticks in people's minds as what alchemy was. It still is an exciting concept, fascinating yet impossible to modern minds, because we know all the reasons why it supposedly cannot happen.

Alchemists may very well have made gold from other elements, and we might duplicate their accomplishments if we could understand what they were trying to communicate in their incomprehensible "recipes." But alchemy was much more than making gold.

In the literature of the time, alchemy was referred to as "The Art." Historical literature contains terminology referring to changes and transformations of one thing into another. The records of alchemical pursuits are incomplete, and we may never know for certain what knowledge was gained by those who devoted their lives to its study. But alchemy was certainly a universal concept, and alchemical literature is found in the records of China, India, Egypt, Greece, Arabia, and Europe.

Western conventional science has conditioned our culture to reject the alchemists' strange symbols and methods of "chemistry" as nonsense, to encourage us to chuckle at the absurdities of magic, to scorn our intuition and call it superstition, and to deny the unexplained.

If, however, you read the works of the great thinkers who have established themselves in learned disciplines such as psychology, mathematics, and physics, you sometimes hear the most superstitious-sounding talk.

For example, in the 1940s Swiss psychoanalyst and psychologist Carl Jung challenged his colleagues with a theory that no one, then or now, seems to know what to do with.

Jung theorized that there was an inherited disposition, a "collective unconscious," available to humans of all ages. He developed this theory because of the symbolic illustrations that alchemists used to explain their theories and concepts. The images Jung's patients dreamed were sometimes quite fantastic and strange, but they bore a striking resemblance to historical alchemical drawings. How could it be explained by coincidence that over and over again, he heard descriptions of similar images from patients he treated, people who had absolutely no knowledge of the obscure drawings from centuries ago?

Could Jung have been theorizing about a universal energy "bank" which is available to all who become receptive? We wish for more brilliant, accepting thinkers like Jung here in the West, to pursue this intriguing theory.

A contemporary Western thinker, Stephen W. Hawking, is searching for a unified theory which will explain everything in the universe. In his 1988 book A *Brief History of Time*, he discussed concepts that, to our way of thinking, go far beyond the physical plane or reality we can perceive with our senses. Among many other fantastic and complex theories, Hawking mentions the string theory, which considers at least ten dimensions of space-time instead of the usual four, and that time travel might be achieved by taking a short-cut through another dimension. Hawking wants to know, "What is it that breathes fire into the equations and makes a universe for them to describe?"* We and many others share his quest for this primal life force.

We reject the explanation of Western science, which grudgingly gives the alchemists of the past credit for beginning the study of chemistry as we know it today, but largely discards their work as nonsense. We believe differently. We believe that alchemy was and is the art which at its heart seeks the things a student of this book seeks: to understand the relationship of humanity to the cosmos, and how to evoke transmutation from one state to another through changes in energy.

Retaining Chi Within Your Body

Most of us lose chi constantly. Here are three basic techniques that the beginning student can safely use to help retain the energy generated by meditation. More advanced energy work is possible only after careful study and practice, preferably under expert, individualized supervision.

An Energy Bridge

Kechari mudra is quite simple and effective in joining the energy meridians or pathways that run through the body. It is performed by pressing the tip of the tongue up to the roof of the mouth. Your goal will be to press your tongue back as far as possible without straining. Like any muscle, your tongue will become more flexible with time and practice. Kechari mudra can be performed with any

* Stephen W. Hawking, A *Brief History of Time*. NY: Bantam Books, 1988. Page 174.

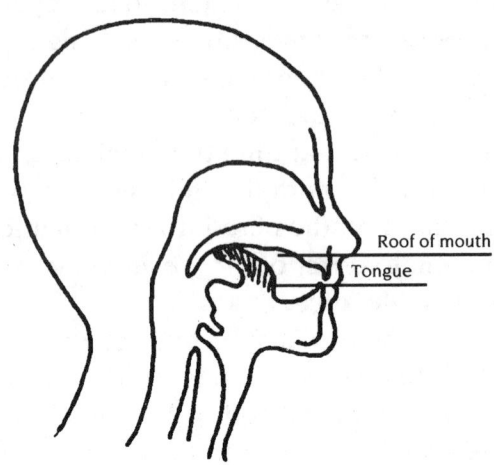

Kechari Mudra

meditation. For some, it is an old friend to turn to during the day. It can help your mind and body do a better job of any task you ask of yourself.

Two Energy Locks

Moola bandha (root lock) helps prevent the loss of chi from the base of the body. To perform it, simply tighten your perineal (anal) muscles. Using it with an inhalation pumps energy upward, so it also functions as a circulator of chi as well as a lock. Use Moola bandha with your breath, inhaling as you tighten the perineal muscles, then exhaling as you relax them. This root lock can be maintained at all times to retain valuable chi.

Jalhandhara bandha (chin lock) diverts chi back down your body, and can be used whenever you wish to contain the energy you have generated. It is performed by tucking your chin firmly into your throat notch. Inhale, tuck in your chin firmly, and hold. Relax and release the lock, then exhale. Do not inhale or exhale while holding the lock itself.

Releasing Excess Energy

Feeling shaky and exhilarated is an indication that you have at least enough, and perhaps too much, built-up energy. Either stop the practice session for the day, or relieve the intensity through a releasing exercise such as the following:

> Stand — barefoot, if possible — on Mother Earth and place both of your hands over Manipura, your solar plexus. (This will be discussed further in the section on chakras.) For now, place your hands just under your rib cage. Women should balance their feminine energy by placing their masculine (right) hand underneath their left. Men should balance their masculine energy by placing their left or feminine hand underneath their right.

> Breathe in, with no locks, imagining blue light coming into Manipura. Breathe out, visualizing blue light moving down the meridians of your legs through the chakra points in the soles of your feet, and into the earth.

> Do this three or four times, until the intensity of energy is calmed to the point where you feel vitally alive, but serene and peaceful.

Trust Builds Belief

Chi is the utilization of the life force within your body, and the quest for it has to be based on trust. In fact, if the words hadn't become disreputable because of their association with the Judeo-Christian religious ethic, you could say that developing chi is an "act of faith." The only way you can progress in developing chi is to convince yourself that it is there, that you visualize it, that you feel it, and that you believe in it — only then will it become truly manifest.

Releasing Excess Energy

The Complete Breath

Our lives depend on oxygen. We can live for many days without food, a few days without water — and scant minutes without air.

The human lung transfers oxygen in and carbon dioxide out of the bloodstream by dispersing air into a system of tiny air sacs. There are several hundred thousand of them in each lung. The actual exchange occurs quickly because each inhaled breath spreads over the large surface of the air sacs.

The lungs pump air in, absorbing oxygen and expelling carbon dioxide, about 16 to 20 times per minute in an adult. Children run and jump and play, and breathe deeply. But on the average, the amount of air you take in and out with each breath will decrease by 45 percent between age 30 and age 75. Because of this, the volume of oxygen going into the blood also decreases by about half.

Our lungs lose elasticity and fail to expand fully, and the rib cage becomes less flexible. For these reasons, the lungs become constricted. The extremities of the lungs then tend to become clogged through the accumulation of toxins because they no longer function optimally. Gradually, the surface area decreases.

Do our bodies warn us of this gradual loss of breathing function? Probably not in ways that will get our immediate attention. The physical body does not deal well with gradual decay. Aging is the deadliest disease of all, because it sneaks up on us throughout a lifetime, until it cannot be denied.

It is clear that any kind of physical exercise will help the lungs, because it forces them to work harder, to fill more deeply, and therefore to get some much needed expansion and contraction.

More important than the oxygen coming in is that each breath brings in chi, the life energy. The more complete the breath, the more vitalizing chi is drawn inward. If you only take half a breath, it follows that you are only half alive. Learn to breathe completely in passive or dynamic meditation, and your lungs will function more effectively the rest of the time.

THE COMPLETE BREATH TECHNIQUE

Sit in a comfortable position, keeping your spine reasonably straight. Relax. Slowly and deeply inhale through your nose. Fill your lungs with air by letting your diaphragm push down on your stomach area, which will expand outward and down. Fill from the bottom of your lungs upward, arching slightly back at the waist as your ribs expand and rise. Take in as much air as is comfortably possible, but do not strain.

Hold this inhalation for a while. When you just begin to feel uncomfortable, take a quick, small sniff of air, then exhale the breath calmly and completely. Your diaphragm will return to its normal position, your stomach will flatten, and your rib cage will fall inward and down.

The small sniff of air assists in a controlled release, which is very important. The key words here are slow, measured, and controlled. In your inhalation and exhalation, nothing is rushed and nothing is strained.

A word of caution: Do not overextend your lungs at first by taking in too much air. If you have been breathing shallowly for years, like most of us, there are areas of your lungs that have not been used for a long time. When these unused portions start expanding with oxygen, there may be some discomfort, so take it slowly. If you have high blood pressure, do the procedure without holding your breath at all. Eliminate that part and you'll still receive the benefits of the slow and complete inhalation and exhalation.

Practise the technique at least six times every morning, and whenever your energy is low. It's excellent when you are tired and dragging and can't stop to rest. You can do it standing, also, if you need. Remember not to strain, and keep the inhalations and exhalations slow, controlled, and as complete as possible. This technique is excellent to regain emotional control. Try it for several minutes if you feel fearful, angry, or sad.

The Complete Breath:
Give yourself the gift of total Life.

The Cleansing Breath

At the end of an exercise or meditation session, try to give your lungs a good cleansing of air and toxins. The following technique helps you get all your breath out, and is good daily practice.

THE CLEANSING BREATH TECHNIQUE

This is best done in a kneeling position in which you can bend forward freely. Place your hands on your stomach, left hand over right, just underneath your rib cage. Bend forward and gently press out all the air by pulling in with your hands and expelling all the air in your lungs.

Then, take a complete breath in about six or seven good-sized sniffs, going back each time until you are sitting upright on your heels. Your diaphragm will expand downward as your lungs fill, your stomach will push outward, and your rib cage will come up. Don't hold this large breath more than a few seconds. Release it explosively, all at once, through your nose.

Assist the rapid and complete cleansing by pulling in with your hands and by leaning forward as you exhale to get all the air out.

Up to seven cleansing breaths can be done at one sitting. This cleansing breath technique is beneficial to anyone, especially for those exposed to a polluted environment (which does include most of us).

The following technique is a breath-balancer which can be performed before any exercise.

Nadi Soghana

The purpose of this "breath of union" is for you to begin to breathe equally through both nostrils. It is an effective technique for balancing the energy in your body and the two hemispheres of your brain, to help you attain a more balanced state of awareness.

To begin with, sit on the floor, cross-legged if possible, or in another comfortable meditation posture. Your left hand, with thumb and index fingers joined, rests on your left knee. The index finger of your right hand rests on your forehead, between your eyebrows at the third eye chakra. The thumb of your right hand will be used to close your right nostril and the middle finger will close your left nostril.

You will probably be breathing through one nostril more than the other. For the purpose of these instructions, we will call the right nostril the dominant one. If you find you are breathing more from the left nostril, begin the breathing sequence in reverse of what we describe, starting out with your left hand closing your nostrils, and so on.

To begin with Nadi Soghana, inhale and press your right nostril (or whichever is your dominant nostril) closed with your right thumb, and exhale forcefully through your left nostril. Inhale through your left nostril as you count to seven. Now close your left nostril with your middle finger of your right hand, and hold your breath again for a count of seven.

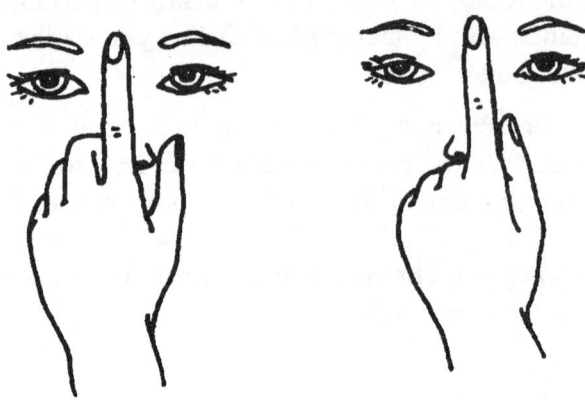

Nadi Soghana

Release your right nostril and exhale through it for a count of seven. Immediately, still keeping your left nostril closed, inhale slowly through your right nostril for a count of seven. Assume Moola bandha as you make this slow inhalation. After you count to seven, close both nostrils and hold your breath for another count of seven. Now release the left nostril and exhale through your left nostril for a count of seven, releasing Moola bandha as you do so.

Repeat the entire sequence seven times in all. Remember, do not hold your breath if you have high blood pressure. You will still gain a balancing benefit from this technique.

Chakras

Everything is energy. You can facilitate the entrance of energy into your body through the top of your head. Here is one way to start learning how to consciously absorb the life force:

RECEIVING THE LIGHT

Sit quietly and close your eyes. Imagine warm white or blue light glowing about six inches above the top of your head. Open your head to receive the light, which flows down your legs, down your arms, and out of you. Then become filled to overflowing simply by closing your fingers and toes so the chi builds inside you. Become saturated, even to the outside of your aura, the field of energy that surrounds every organism. Become replete with energy. Take your time. Then let the light grow until it surrounds you. Notice how you feel. When you are ready, open your eyes. The protection of the light will remain with you.

Chakras: Spinning Energy Wheels

For thousands of years, Eastern philosophers have believed that the human organism gets most of its energy from invisible waves or rays entering through the top of the head. Every parent knows the soft spot on a baby's head, the fontanelle, must be protected for the child's first months of life. The bones of the skull naturally close this opening with age, to protect the delicate brain tissues. Just as this opening is thought to have received energy from the mother while she holds her child in the womb, Eastern tradition teaches that the crown of the head remains the primary entrance place of vital chi throughout life. In addition, significant amounts of chi also come up through the spine and through the feet, from Mother Earth.

As the life force enters the body, it passes through and activates the seven primary chakras. The word chakra means "wheel," and is an ancient East Indian symbol, used in this sense to mean a center of physical and psychic energy. The seven major chakras are known by many different names. We prefer the East Indian terms:

1. Muladhara
2. Svadhisthana

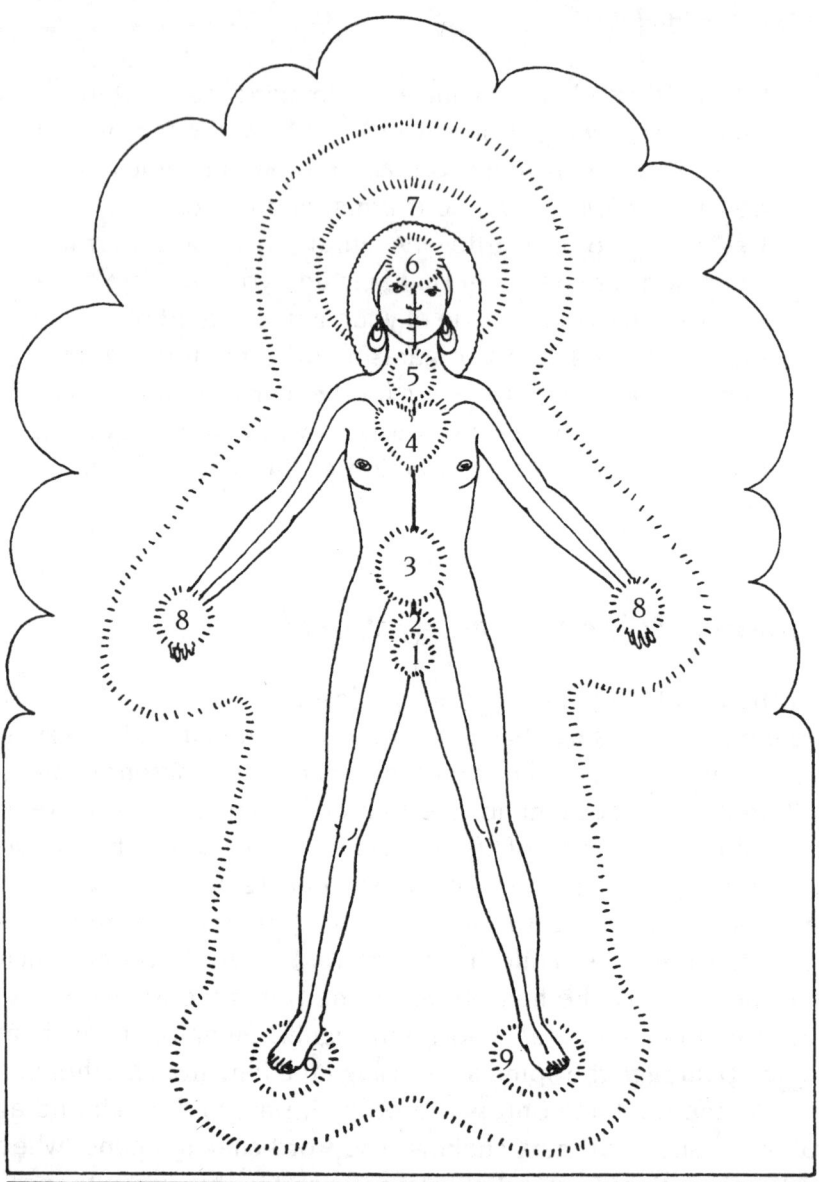

1. **Muladahara**	2. **Svadhisthana**	3. **Manipura**
4. **Anahata**	5. **Vishudha**	6. **Ajna**
7. **Sahasrara**	8. **Lao Kun**	9. **Yung Chuan**

The Chakras

3. Manipura

4. Anahata

5. Vishudha

6. Ajna

7. Sahasrara

Also indicated on the accompanying chakra diagram are two secondary chakras. We like to call the palm chakra (8) by its Chinese name, Lao Kun, and we refer to the chakra in the soles of the feet (9) as Yung Chuan, "Bubbling Spring." We mention these secondary chakras in some of the dynamic meditations in Part Two, for example in Red Dragon Chi Kung, where pyramids are formed between the chakras.

There are, of course, many other energy points and junctions along the energy meridians (which correspond to our nervous system) which lace our bodies. The acupuncturist uses these points to cure illness and relieve pain.

The major chakras are located along the spinal column, and are closely related to the endocrine system, the nervous system, and the circulatory system, all of which influence hormonal secretions in some way. The accompanying illustration shows approximately where the chakras are located, and you can see for yourself how they relate to the diagrams of body systems.

At the peak of health and vitality, our chakras spin or vibrate at great speed. As we grow older or develop unhealthy habits and begin to lose vitality, the rate of vibration of some or all of the chakras slows down. This gradual decrease in vibration affects the flow of hormones released by the endocrine system. Too much, too little — either condition brings on the familiar symptoms of aging, and also increases the possibility of disease.

Your task is to mix and balance the incoming energy, the earth energy, with the energy coming in from the universe, and to create a system of chakras that literally "hums." If balance occurs, each chakra will be open, the physical body will perform optimally, and a unified organism will result.

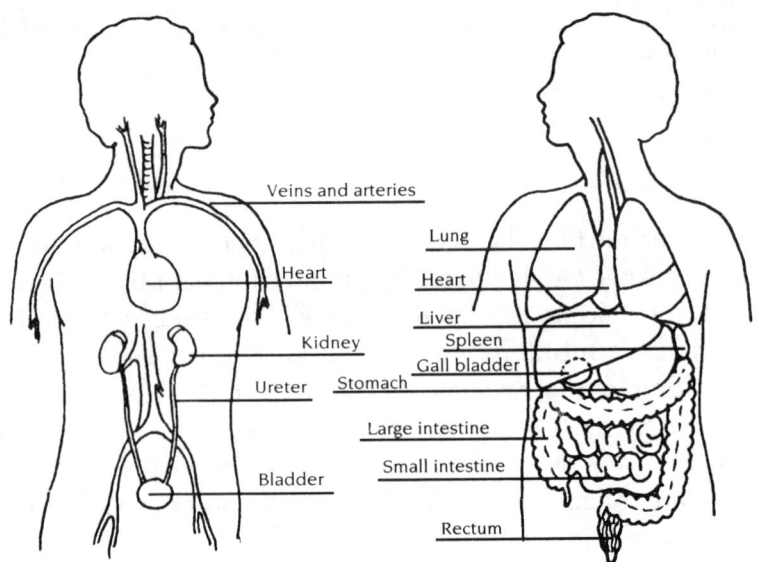

The Circulatory System   The Major Organs

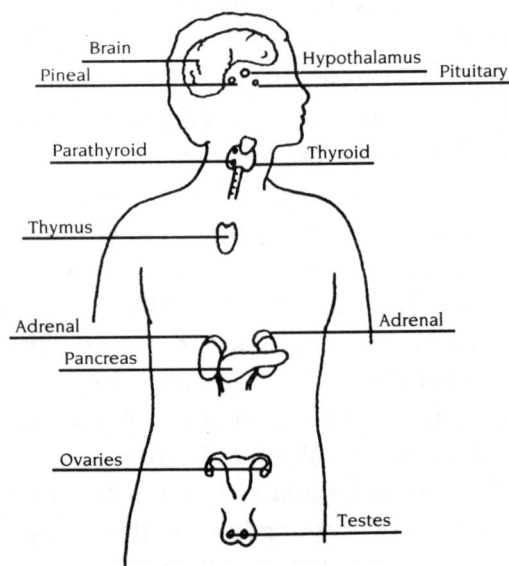

The Endocrine System

Body Systems

Are You "In the Pink"?

When concentrating on the different chakra centers of your body, you may see certain colors when your eyes are closed. Once your goals become more spiritual, you may feel drawn toward particular colors, depending on the chakra you are working with. It is all a matter of what feels right to you at each particular stage of your spiritual development.

Rainbow colors are almost universally accepted to represent the chakra centers, although there is not total agreement as to which color symbolizes which chakra. But this does not point to one being right and one being wrong; rather, it points to the difference in what color was seen by a particular master while in meditation.

The number of light waves that come to our eyes each second is known as the frequency of light. The different frequencies are perceived as different colors. The red end of the light spectrum, or rainbow, is the lowest frequency of light waves. The blue end is the highest frequency.

And, of course, light is not the only thing that has a frequency because it is composed of waves of energy. All parts of the universe, flesh and blood, plant and mineral, vibrate because each is a different form of energy. Our chakras are concentrations of energy which seem to have their own integrity, and their own separate identity and frequency. You can "feel" someone behind you without actually hearing, seeing, or noticing him or her in any way other than identifying a field of energy that is vibrating a bit differently than your energy body.

We are presenting the color scheme and key words we are most comfortable with, based on the colors our energy work has shown us. You can adapt it according to what colors you identify with when working with each chakra.

Chakra Colors and Keywords

Muladhara	Red	The base chakra, relating to survival and procreation
Svadhistana	Orange	The health and pleasure chakra, relating to well-being, immunity from disease, and pleasure in life
Manipura	Yellow	The power chakra or solar plexus, relating to a reservoir of spiritual and physical energy which gives strength to all the other chakras and keeps them healthy
Anahata	Green	The heart chakra, relating to unconditional acceptance which frees the other chakras from ego, melds our heart's love energy with cosmic wisdom, and makes the bridge from physical to spiritual and from known to unknown
Vishudha	Blue	The throat chakra, relating to creativity and self-expression, the gateway to communication with the unknown
Ajna	Violet	The third eye chakra, relating to intuition, paranormal powers, and psychic awareness
Sahasrara	Indigo	The crown chakra, relating to liberation into the cosmic realm, bliss

Develop Patience

Here in the West, we are competitive and impatient, attributes which do not promote spiritual development. We want to work in the stars because it sounds more interesting, more exciting; it is something new and different. English words tend to give false impressions, because of how we use the same words in everyday life. Without thinking about it, we want to rush on to do "advanced work" because it must be more important than "beginning work." And, of course, violet is a royal color and must therefore be more deserving of our concentration than plain old red!

It is important not to make the mistake of confusing the terms "higher" and "better." Muladhara, Svadhisthana, and Manipura are known as the earth-based chakras. Vishudha, Ajna, and Sahasrara are the cosmic chakras. Right now, most of us are living in the physical plane and our firm foundation, our base, is very well-developed. But the earth-based chakras all need nourishment and attention. At the same time that you are developing the chakras that are symbolically higher in the body and which deal more with the spiritual aspects of life, give your three lower chakras nourishment. Try not to forget that while we are on the physical plane, even though our heads may be in the clouds, our feet are still on the ground.

Props

Especially for the beginner, external props help create an environment conducive to passive or dynamic meditation. They are important in defining a familiar space, where we not so much withdraw from the world as step aside, into calmer water, out of the swiftly flowing, erratic, and stimulating stream of modern life.

In the theater, props are simply objects used to help create a realistic effect as a backdrop to the actors. We are expanding the term here to indicate things like color and lighting, jewelry, clothing, and music. These tangible elements can help set the stage for spiritual growth. The repeated use of props also conditions you to being prepared fully, in body and in mind, to dwell for a space in the realm of the spirit.

The created environment, however, should not be more important than the inner workings of your body. For some advanced students, external props may be unnecessary, because true spirituality can be achieved even in the midst of chaos. All the settings in the world will not replace what must happen inside. Things must change and grow deep within yourself.

As an example, here is a word picture of one possible ideal situation for spiritual training where external props are important. It is tied to our preferences, but it is general enough for anyone:

> You are ready to go through your individualized exercise system, part of a daily routine of about an hour or so which you have dedicated to your spiritual growth. You are barefoot, outside, your feet on the ground, and you can feel chi flowing into your body from Mother Earth. You are wearing loose clothing of silk and cotton, in the colors that make you feel the best. Your jewelry is gemstones, wooden beads, and gold and silver bangles because they sound and feel good on you and against your skin and hair. Lyrical, haunting tones of music reach your ears as you begin a passive meditation and then your warmup routine. The musical beat changes, becoming a pulsating drumbeat for dynamic meditation. Then, you slow the pace down as the music relaxes into a lyrical, contemplative style to promote cool-down and closing passive meditation. You are at peace.

You do have to be flexible. So, instead of our idyllic example, you may find yourself inside with only a few minutes to spare, in your regular street clothes, with no music — perhaps a disruption of voices, motors, and blaring, unsuitable music may surround you. No matter, through practice, you will continue to make progress, to focus, despite an imperfect environment. Let's look at the various types of external props, and how you can adapt them according to circumstances.

Props:
Consciously choose, with total awareness,
to create a spiritual space.

Indoors and Outdoors

The stimulating influence of natural sunlight, with its full spectrum of wavelengths, helps combat low energy. After a period of sunless days, you will automatically want to be in the sunlight when the weather breaks. During the winter, especially on cloudy days, if the normal seasonal slowing of your body has left you not just less energetic but actually depressed, spending several hours each day in brilliant artificial light will help provide some of the same benefits as being outside in bright sunlight.

Actually, it can be lovely inside, where you have more control over the environment. Our planet is sadly overpopulated and getting more so all the time. Humans are also curious creatures and are afraid of what is different. Because others may not understand, they are sometimes fearful and even angry; you may have to adapt to local customs by going indoors.

The weather is often better inside, also. Whatever the reason that brings you indoors, you will want to recreate the feelings of openness, light, and contact with Mother Earth. Always try to do meditations barefoot or in socks. Dim lighting can be draining, so keep the area brightly lit. A southern window may let in enough light during the day for exercises without additional artificial lighting. In the evening or late afternoon, you will need to supplement with good artificial lights. A few luxuriant house plants can help bring the spirit of the outdoors inside, and will also freshen your air.

When staying indoors for your spiritual work, however, remember that you are losing two benefits: the nurturing influence of sunlight, and direct contact of your body with the earth. Sometimes you can get along without these benefits as you generate and maintain chi in your body. At other times, you may feel that direct contact with the open sky and with Mother Earth is vital. So then, you should go outside, even if it is only to sit and meditate for a few minutes, breathing deeply.

Colors, Clothing, and Scents

Different colors can be used to achieve certain responses. Physical responses to color are not tied to our individual psyches or bear much relation to our cultural background. In fact, everyone has the same general physical response to certain colors. Greens and blues and pinks are quieting, reds and oranges and yellows are stimulating, and white can be draining.

Even colorblind individuals, who cannot identify the color itself, react in the same way to these colors. So although the mechanism of how subtle vibrational energies such as color and light affect us is not completely understood, this influence is well-documented.

The section dealing with chakras gives an interpretation of colors as they relate to aspects of the total self. Each chakra and its related color needs attention. From time to time, you will find a natural affinity for certain frequencies of color, because each color vibrates with one or more of the chakra centers. Your body will begin to respond to the color of the chakra you are developing, and if you are attentive to your body's language you will be able to detect this response. You can choose to focus on a particular color and incorporate it in clothing, jewelry, and accessories. Indulge yourself where possible, and let the colors vibrate and accentuate your presence in the moment.

Paying attention to how certain colors and fabrics feel develops awareness and is a form of spiritual training, a turning inward. We have been drawn to the colors violet and fuchsia for the last few years. When we can't find what we want, we purchase plain white cotton clothing and dye it ourselves.

Natural fabrics look good and feel good; silk is believed to protect your aura. Cotton and wool also make excellent clothing. Whatever you wear, give yourself a chance to become accustomed to it before you decide if it's good for you or not. Soon, you may find that most synthetic fabrics just don't "feel" right.

Generally, the clothes you wear should have been bought by you, new. But we often acquire used clothing via second-hand clothing stores and yard sales. Sometimes this is the best way to find affordable silk clothing. These garments most probably have energy vibrations from the previous owner which could conflict with your own energy body. To remove the unwanted vibrations from the fabric, wash the clothing with a high-quality soap and rinse it with water that has vinegar added, and an infusion of rosemary or another cleansing herb. Then, without using a dryer, hang it outdoors (turned inside out to prevent fading) and let the sun cleanse it further. It is also a good idea to have sachets of protective herbs, such as lavender and rosemary, in your closets and dresser drawers.

If you like incense, by all means use it. Experiment with other natural aromas, like crushed mint or fresh flowers. You can also use vanilla and almond extract as a perfume. To remove unwanted odors in rooms, instead of just covering them as commercial air fresheners do, prepare a mist bottle with plain water and a little rose or lavender water, or lemon juice. Spray this toward the ceiling and let the water droplets "rain" down, pulling offensive odors down and out of the air. It's almost as refreshing as the rain-washed outdoors.

Gemstones, Crystals, and Metals

Various metals and precious and semi-precious stones are believed to hold magical properties of healing, according to each metal or stone's unique capabilities. Men and women alike should feel free to expand their jewelry and adornment selections according to these traditional beliefs.

Only a few examples will be given here. If this becomes an area of great interest to you, we advise you to consult one of the many excellent books on the subject.

Gemstones for Each Chakra

Muladhara	Garnet, Black onyx	A grounding influence, helps base center to be healthy
Svadhistana	Amber, Carnelian	Helps balance your attitude toward pleasure
Manipura	Topaz, Citrine	Helps strengthen the power center

Anahata	Rose quartz, Pink and green tourmaline	Heals and helps to open the heart center
Vishudha	Turquoise, Aquamarine	Aids in channelling creativity and verbal communication
Ajna	Amethyst	Helps clear channels between the conscious and subconscious and aids intuition
Sahasrara	Diamond, Clear quartz	Assists in connecting your vibrational level with the infinite

(Diamonds of low quality can have negative effects on your body; an excellent quality quartz crystal would be preferable.)

Metals

Gold: Warming, strengthening, masculine; associated with the sun and fire; a gold ring worn on the middle finger strengthens fire and accentuates the masculine.

Silver: Cooling, calming, feminine; associated with the moon and the sea; a silver ring worn on the index finger emphasizes the feminine.

Copper: Associated with Venus and the sea; also emphasizes the feminine.

A bracelet made of a strand each of gold (or brass as an acceptable substitute), silver, and copper is said to be healing and balancing. If you wear a certain metal and it feels uncomfortable or leaves a stain on your skin, you probably have enough of that element in your body and should not wear it.

Any crystal or article of jewelry should be cleansed after purchase and periodically cleansed thereafter. Leave it covered with salt for two or three days and then set it in direct sunlight for a few hours. Then you might wish to place it overnight with some of your other crystals and sacred spiritual objects, to allow for attunement to your energy body.

Pay especially close attention to your inner feelings as you explore various gems and metals. Hold a piece in your hands and try to be totally open and aware of what your intuition tells you.

Music

For many people, background music is the most important prop for setting a personal spiritual stage. It is wonderful to have a wide selection available.

Cassette tapes are still our favorite, because with a small battery-operated tape player, you can take your music with you almost anywhere. It is the most adaptable and inexpensive method of having the spiritual scene set with music.

If you don't already have anything suitable, we suggest you consult your local music dealer for some ideas on which music to select. Listen to several examples of New Age music, of Native American flute music, of drumming music. You'll need at least two different styles, so plan on making at least two tape selections initially.

You'll need music with a regular, pulsating beat. It should be compelling, invigorating — the music should urge you to move. This type of music will be necessary for dynamic meditations like Red Dragon Chi Kung and Earth Dancing.

The other type of background music, for use with the slightly slower pace of T'ai Chi Chi Kung, for example, needs to be relaxing and peaceful. This style of music will be calmer and will have a slower tempo. We have given some suggestions in the Appendix.

In general, music with a tempo or regular beat at 60 beats per minute will work for all the exercises. This maintains a relaxed heart rate. Studies have shown that music at this tempo can help lower blood pressure, steady irregular heart rhythms, and even soothe migraine headaches.

Anyone can learn to beat a drum. If you get a chance, try one out. Those who become proficient seem to be able to lose themselves in the rhythm, to reach their own meditative state while drumming, as well as provide a stimulating accompaniment for any kind of exercise. You can learn to make your own drums from hollowed-out tree sections, using prepared hides or ones you have prepared yourself. As usual, what you get out of drumming is in direct proportion to how much of yourself you put into it.

Internal Tools

For organizational purposes we have found it necessary to group these elements together and give them a heading which is somewhat misleading. Everything we have presented so far deals in some way with the process of internalization, which is necessary to achieve spiritual growth. Here, we briefly deal with visualization, with mantras and yantras, and with koans, not because they are not important in their own right, but because we cannot discuss everything in one book. In one manner of thinking, every element, every tool we discuss is an internal aid toward one goal: reaching a meditative state. Each one is a subject for an entire book, and we hope you will research further into each as you find the time to do so.

Visualization

The process of creating pictures in your mind is the conscious use of your imagination to achieve desired goals. In the dream state, we visualize completely, inserting ourselves into our imagination so that all our external senses appear to function and we truly believe in what is happening. How real it appears depends on your point of view regarding what reality is.

The cultivation of chi begins with imagination. Through creative visualization, your mind has something to focus on, to begin to move energy. This movement starts as a pretense, a picture in your mind. For example, imagining chi as a thin blue stream moving and rising up from your solar plexus to the crown of your head and back down your spine is a standard visualization that works for many people. By recreating the sensations of smell, hearing, and touch along with sight, your awareness of chi flow will increase. After practice, this kind of mental activity produces a physical response, and thus chi flow moves from pretense to reality.

Beyond seeing something in your mind, you can aid your imagination by tracing the energy path with your hand. This actively involves the sense of touch and is helpful to some people. Going one step further, you can create a sensation of internal "touching" by coordinating visualization with breath. As you breathe in slowly, draw energy up your spine. As you breathe out, let the energy return to the base. Yet another way to use the sense of touch is to moisten your finger with saliva and then touch the skin over one of your chakra centers. You can also simply hold your fingers there. Both will help you focus on the chakra center.

We use visualization for several purposes, often at the same time. Visualization is used to help generate chi flow, to distract our logic circuits so we can become more creative, or to prepare our mind to accept meditation. We often use it combined with breath and colors to help create the space for the reality of inner movement to occur.

Mantras, Yantras, and Koans

A tool of passive meditation is the mantra, or chant. These ancient combinations of sounds may be repeated over and over out loud, or to yourself, to help reach a meditative space. They are sacred sounds which stimulate certain chakra centers dependent on the frequency of their vibration. You should find the pitches that seem to feel most comfortable and seem to resonate within your body. Try changing where you sing them occasionally, because new placements may be necessary as your chakras fluctuate and balance. For more exploration of mantras and their effects, you may want to attend workshops, or obtain cassette tapes and videotapes on the subject. Then you will be able to chant along and know that you have the correct intervals and tempo.

Om na - ma shi - va. Om na - ma -a shi - va   ya.

Om na - ma shi - va. Om na - ma shi - va.

Pronounced "Om nah-mah she-vah. Om nah-mah she-vah-yah. Om nah-mah she-vah." This is a purifying chant that translates as "I honor the divine within."

Ga - te,   ga - te,   pa - ra - ga - te,   pa - ra - sam-ga-te,

bod - hi   va - ha.

Pronounced "Gah-tey, gah-tey, pah-rah-gah-tey, pah-rah-sahm-gah-tey, bow-dee swah-hah." Paraphrased as "Gone, gone, beyond all illusions of the physical plane, on the breath."

Aum ma - ni pad-me hum. Aum ma - ni pad-me hum.

Pronounced "Ah-om mah-ney pahd-may hoom." Paraphrased as "Male and female energies in a state of balance."

Mantras

Yantras are traditional sacred designs or pictures. They are symbolic drawings which have a center or focus point which is empty, representing the concept of bindu. Bindu is the spark, the beginning, and the totality of the entire universe. The yantra is placed at eye level and meditated upon to help attain spiritual awareness.

In Part Three in the section on Anahata, the heart chakra, we give an example of a yantra. The use of yantras is quite involved and complex, and is beyond the scope of this book. Please research this topic further if you are interested.

Koans, from the Zen tradition, are yet another technique to aid in meditation. A koan is a question that appears to have no answer. It is designed to baffle your logical mind so that you can move into a state of meditation. You can contemplate a koan at any time during the day, or you can think of it during any form of passive meditation, Here are three koans we like:

1. What is my original face, the face I had before my parents were born?

2. What is the sound of one hand clapping?

3. Who am I?

Meditation

Actions on the physical plane can only be explained using words, and words cannot really describe or explain what meditation is. True meditation, in our understanding, is being totally in the moment, outside of past and future.

Have you ever sat around a campfire with good friends, sharing good conversation? You may have noticed that occasionally all conversation ceases, and a comfortable silence takes hold. As you gaze into the flames, your mind wanders as it is both tied down and released at the same time by the fascinating, dancing, glowing

Breath	Candle	Mirror	Yantra	Mantra

Meditation

vision before you. At such a time, your logical mind might relax into a creative state which may produce new insights and conversations. But during some of the silences, you may have slipped into a true meditative state, where you simply are not holding any conscious thought in your mind at all.

What we call the physical plane is the actual reality of daily life, and it is dependent upon concepts of the past and the future for its existence. The very dirt we stand upon is the geologic past — and our next breath is our future. Meditation is the search for our own eternal inner present.

We believe that meditation is a space in which you attempt to temporarily step away from the bonds of the brain. The brain is simply a fleshy computer, a useful implement for our souls while we are abiding in the physical plane.

We are much more than this physical brain. We tend to forget (do we forget, or does our brain just forget?) this fact and become slaves to this physical computer, "thinking" that is all we are. The brain is necessary and helpful at times, of course, but in meditation the goal is to rest the brain while still being totally aware through that part of us that is metaphorically bigger than the brain, outside of what the brain deals with. This is difficult to accomplish because the brain is a spoiled tyrant that does not give up control easily. We must trick it into letting go.

Left Mode, Right Mode

It is generally accepted that in most people one half of the brain gives us the ability to perceive logically, in an orderly manner, and to communicate verbally with others. Much of our thinking and self-awareness is tied to language, so the half of the brain, or hemisphere, which deals with verbal processes tends to dominate in most of us. We call this hemisphere of the brain the left mode.

The other hemisphere of the brain, the right mode, deals with nonverbal processes like the appreciation of music, intuitive leaps of logic, and imaging or visualizing which gives proficiency in art. It is where we dream, and where we understand metaphors such as connecting the motion of a chiffon veil with the lyrical qualities of a haunting melody.

In most of us, the control of the right hand and the right side of our body is generated from the left side of our brain; the left mode. If this side of the brain should become injured or incapacitated, for example through stroke or accidental damage, the right side of the body would be most severely impacted. Conversely, the left side of the body would be most affected by injuries to the right side of the brain.

It is also interesting that for those left-handers whose mother was also left-handed, it appears that the traditional left mode processing is switched and comes from the opposite side of the brain than the rest of us. In this case, the control of the right hand and right side would generate from the right hemisphere of the brain, and traditional left mode processing would occur in the left hemisphere.

The difference between the two hemispheres is important to our discussion here because it points to an important concept: at least two major types of physiological information processing occur, to some degree, in each human being. One side is not more advanced than the other, as has been thought in the past, but each perceives reality differently. Each hemisphere or mode appears to have its own separate experience of an event, to separately react in an emotional way, and to separately receive and interpret data. A thick network of nerves, of energy pathways, connects the two halves of our brain, and seems to provide the physical link so a smooth interaction between the two usually occurs.

It will be the subject of an upcoming book of ours, this relationship between left and right mode, how it relates to the state of meditation, and how it relates to Anahata, the heart chakra. For now, we leave you with the thought that these things are both of the world of conventional medicine and of the world of spirit. Indeed, the concept of unity, of interrelatedness, the holistic view of this earth and the universe, is a right mode concept. Do all you can to cultivate the expression of your right mode's reality.

Passive Techniques for Spiritual Growth

As with all spiritual concepts, there are no clear beginnings and endings. So it is with the many passive and active techniques which are traditional pathways to understanding your spirituality. We refer to these techniques as "meditations." The term is used here to include a broad category of exercises which deal with the movement of energy; with centering, focusing, and controlling the mind and body; and with attaining a true meditative state. Some techniques are less active than others, and we will discuss them first.

A basic passive technique is to watch your breath. Sit comfortably and focus on the breath going in and out of your nostrils. Consciously feel the sensation of air going in through your nose as you inhale. As you exhale, consciously feel the air going out.

The use of the word "consciously" means that you try to be aware on all sensory levels possible. Concentrate on the sensation of the cool inhalation and then the warm exhalation, and/or visualize a colored light or mist being inhaled and exhaled. Once again, we can get tangled up in what different words mean, because for some people, the terms "visualization" and "sensation" mean virtually the same thing when working with energy and meditation. Just be sure that you involve yourself totally in whatever mental imagery/visualization/sensation you use.

Another passive meditation technique is to sit with your eyes closed, a few feet away from a blank wall. You are placing yourself in a non-reactive physical setting so that you may more easily turn inward.

Sometimes it can be useful to give your eyes stimulation, such as by gazing softly into a mirror. You are not actually looking at yourself so much as you are looking past yourself into infinity. You might also try looking at a candle flame, letting your vision blur slightly as you unfocus your eyes and become lost in the flame. With these kinds of passive meditations, you may also wish to incorporate mantras, yantras, and koans, as discussed in the previous section.

Mudras

Mudras are gestures made with the hands that help direct and focus energy in specific ways during meditation. There are different meanings of the word, and there are different interpretations of the various mudras themselves. There are mudras which use parts of the body other than the hands, such as Kechari mudra with the tongue, which we discussed earlier.

We are giving you a few of the hand mudras. A brief explanation of each is given, but it is up to you to experiment with them and discover which works best. You may find, as we have done, that you will use certain mudras for certain applications and not for others. As always, be aware of your changing needs.

The following hand mudras can be assumed at the start of any passive meditation and continued throughout to help direct energy. Each hand and finger has a traditional esoteric symbolism. This symbolism varies somewhat according to different customs and systems. Here, we suggest that the right hand symbolizes the sun, and the left mode. The keywords are masculine, verbal, and logical. The left hand symbolizes the moon and the right mode, with keywords of intuitive, non-verbal, and feminine. The thumb is associated with the element ether and the brain meridian. The index finger is associated with the element air and the lung meridian.

To continue with the symbolism, the middle finger represents fire, the intestine meridian, and sexual impulses. The ring finger symbolizes water and the kidney meridian. Lastly, the little finger represents earth and the heart meridian.

Mudra 1: Holding the Mind. Hold your right thumb with your left hand. You are holding the left mode of your brain, your analytical thinking impulses. This will help still your thoughts and achieve a sense of quiet serenity.

Mudra 2: Sun – Moon. Place your left hand, palm down, upon your right hand, which is palm up. This mudra helps bring balance between the dominant and passive halves of your being.

Holding the Mind

Sun – Moon	Fire	Air	The Void

Mudras

Mudra 3: The Void. Place your left hand, palm up, on top of your right hand, which is also palm up. Touch your two thumb tips together, thus linking the meridians of your brain. This mudra, like Sun – Moon, helps to bring balance. It is also very helpful in stilling your mind.

Mudra 4: Fire. Rest your hands, palms up, on your knees. On each hand, touch your middle finger to your thumb.

Mudra 5: Air. Rest your hands, palms up, on your knees. Connect your index fingers with your thumbs.

Whatever methods you use during meditation, it may not be necessary to continue them consciously after you enter a meditative state. After all, these are all means to an end; devices, tools. When using a mantra or a breath visualization, for example, you will probably stop the device naturally once you have entered the space beyond the device. When you are using the technique of actually looking at something — a flame, a mirror, or a sacred drawing — as the watcher you will gradually lose yourself in the image you see, and you and the image will become one. Do not become so dedicated to performing a particular technique that it becomes a hindrance to true meditation. Mudras can usually become established as a habit, so that you maintain them naturally, even during deep meditative states.

Here are two structured passive meditations that we have found effective.

Bringing Up the Light

This is one of our favorite techniques to help create a sense of beauty and serenity. The glowing light of the visualization will generate chi, or prana. The inhalation with Moola bandha sends the energy upwards, and the hands assist in directing the energy. After you conclude, you may find yourself slipping into a meditative state. This exercise is especially helpful after a long day of work. You might take a leisurely bath, put on a minimum of loose clothing, or none at all, and go where you can relax and meditate without interruption.

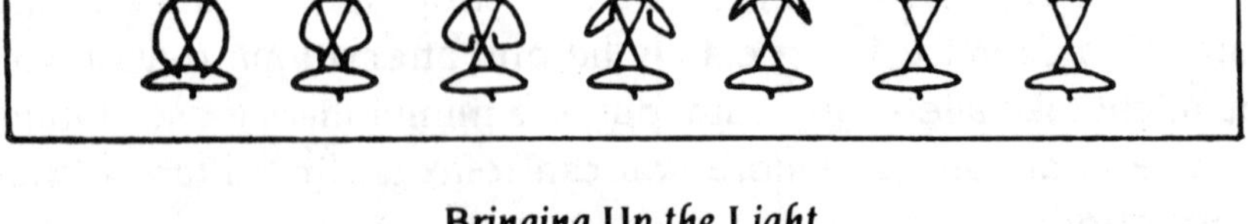

Bringing Up the Light

Sit in a comfortable position with your hands resting lightly on your knees. Placing a pillow beneath your tailbone may help you sit more comfortably. Close your eyes and sit quietly for a few moments, watching your breath. When you feel calm and relaxed, begin the following movement and breath technique.

Inhale with Moola bandha and draw your hands from your knees to the level of Muladhara, the base chakra. Imagine a glowing light filling that chakra. You might also say the name to yourself as you visualize and focus on that particular spot of your body. Hold your breath as long as you comfortably can. Exhale and relax Moola bandha, letting your hands return to rest lightly on your knees. Let the visualization, the glowing light, remain in Muladhara.

Inhale with Moola bandha and draw your hands from your knees to the level of Svadhistana, the health and pleasure chakra. See and feel the glowing, vibrant light filling your being to the level of the second chakra. Hold your breath. Exhale and relax Moola bandha, returning your hands to your knees. The level of the light remains at Svadhistana.

Continue in this same manner through the chakras. Bring the light up to Manipura, the power chakra; Anahata, the heart chakra; Vishudha, the throat chakra; and Ajna, the third eye chakra.

You now have the level of the light up to your brow. Inhale with Moola bandha again and lift your hands up to Sahasrara, the crown chakra, bringing the light all the way up to the top of your head. Then lift your hands further, bringing that brilliant light up over Sahasrara so it suffuses your entire body, and surrounds you in a bright egg of energy.

Exhale and relax. Allow your hands to return to your knees. Breathe naturally and experience your brilliant golden aura which you have filled with chi through Bringing Up the Light.

WOMB MEDITATION

This beautiful meditation teaches without any effort or any attempt at visualization on your part. Simply by performing it, you will create your own internal sacred space.

With this technique, you are voluntarily shutting out external stimuli for a time, while you abide in your own inner space. Your internal senses continue to function. You may see lights or patterns in different colors, hear some of your own internal body processes, or you may hear humming. Some people believe that this is the sound of the flow of the universe. It has been called the "sound of the void," the "cosmic om," or "divine music." Whatever you see or hear, be witness to what you are experiencing, without judging in any way. Try to simply experience this wondrous inner space.

While sitting or lying down comfortably, place your thumbs over the openings of your ears to shut out any external sounds. Place your palms near your cheeks, close your eyes gently, and cover your eyes with your forefingers to shut out any external sights. Let your middle fingers touch on either side of your nostrils to eliminate your sense of smell. Lay your ring fingers on your upper lip and place your little fingers underneath your lower lip, closing your mouth and preventing speech.

Release the pressure on your nostrils and breathe in deeply. Now close off your nostrils and hold your breath for as long as is comfortable. Release the pressure and exhale completely. Inhale again, and hold. Repeat this process as long as you wish.

Experience the womb with awareness
Experience the beauty and silence
Experience the cosmic Mother.

Womb Meditation

The Active Meditation of Sufi Whirling

For most beginners in spiritual work, the best that can be expected is to achieve a sort of preliminary meditative state when using passive meditation techniques. The process of attaining true meditation is that of educating yourself as to what it really is. That is always the difficulty, but as you work diligently, understanding will grow with experience.

For those who want to learn about the meditative state in a more active way, we offer the technique of Sufi Whirling. When performed properly, it is reliable for placing you in a meditative state.

Sufi Whirling is said to have been created by the thirteenth century Sufi master and poet, Mevlana Jalalu-ddin Rumi (September 30, 1207 – December 17, 1273). As the legend goes, one day while in the market place, Rumi began to spin spontaneously. The people watched until it was time to go home that night. When they returned the next day, Rumi was still whirling. He continued whirling for a total of 36 hours, and then the explosion of spiritual enlightenment happened. Whirling is practiced to this day among the Mevlevi Sufis, known as the Whirling Dervishes.

It seems nearly impossible for anyone to hold a thought while whirling; the mind receives a much needed rest. In fact, if you persist in thinking while whirling, you will probably become dizzy. The beauty of whirling is that even if you have had little experience understanding what meditation is and achieving its goals, whirling immediately forces you into the meditative space.

Through Sufi Whirling, and any deep meditation, you can gain a centered, vibrant serenity which can be channeled into all aspects of your life. It seems to be especially helpful for increasing creativity, and when learning something new that you can't seem to grasp.

We do not advise whirling as a daily practice, unless you have already done a great deal of work to open up the channels and balance the chakras in your body. Then you can do as much as seems right for you.

A beginner should limit time spent whirling, as it is such a powerful tool. We suggest no more than about 25 minutes once or twice a week at first. Alternate it with exercises to open the energy

Sufi Whirling:
"La illaha illa'llah."
"There is no god, but God."

channels and chakras during the rest of the week. As always, trust your body's reactions. If you feel nauseous or suffer any other discomforts, stop. If all is well, you could gradually begin to try more whirling. You probably should not whirl for more than 25 minutes at one time, but you may increase the times during the week that you whirl, if it seems beneficial.

THE TECHNIQUE OF SUFI WHIRLING

Ingest nothing for two hours prior to whirling. Stand with your arms by your sides. Your hands should be softly cupped, right hand palm up, left hand palm down, cupping the energy from above and below. Begin to spin slowly, always in a counterclockwise direction. Let your arms float up of their own accord, until when you are going quite fast, they may be up at shoulder level. You must spin in the counterclockwise direction; according to tradition, this relates to the rotational direction of our planet and to the orbit of our solar system around the sun.

You will find that to spin in one place without moving about, your left foot will have to serve as a pivot point, the very center of your foot staying in one place or at least nearly in one place. The ball and heel of your left foot will rotate around the center pivot, and your right foot will rotate around the left at a comfortable distance.

It is very important that your eyes remain unfocused and looking inward, rather than outward. We have seen people whirl with their eyes closed as well; again, do what works for you. If your eyes are unfocused (whether open or closed), with your attention inward, you will begin to forget the outer environment, the body, and the mind — you will just be. If your gaze becomes focused, you will become dizzy. This will cause you to lose the benefits of the whirling, and you may fall.

When you need to stop for any reason, gradually slow down until you come to a stop. Stand until your balance is restored. At this point, you can use the T'ai Chi Chi Kung posture Crane Draws in Chi described in Part Two. Crane Draws in Chi will circulate and balance the powerful energy that has been generated within your being by the whirling, and help you restore your equilibrium.

If you whirl with anyone else present, they must be told to take care to avoid you if they pass nearby. You cannot see them, and even if you do have enough outward focus to do so, you cannot avoid them without losing your balance.

The Zikr or Sufi Mantra

The Sufi mantras, or zikr, consist of repetitive chanting of one of the Moslem names of God. The most commonly used zikr is "La illaha illa'llah," meaning "There is no god, but God." This zikr is a repetition of the negative phrase "La illaha," or "There is no god," followed by the affirmative phrase "illa'llah," or "but God." According to tradition, the negative desire, is replaced with the positive love of God. Our interpretation of "love of God" here is a connection with pure existence.

The Whirling Dervishes traditionally repeat a zikr as they turn, allowing their consciousness to lose itself in the mantra. It is difficult, however, for the beginner to repeat the zikr and whirl simultaneously. An appropriate way to use the traditional technique is for someone else to be chanting the zikr as you whirl. This can be a friend present as you whirl, or you might consider taping a session of chanting with a musical background, to produce a tape to play while you whirl.

La il - la - ha il - la - 'llah, la il - la - ha il - la - 'llah.

Mantra

Pronunciation is self-explanatory. Paraphrased as "There is no god, but God." A zikr or Sufi mantra, to be repeated while performing Sufi Whirling.

A Native American Energy Meditation

The Dance of the Four Directions was taught to us as a Native American way to become centered and balanced. This graceful and beautiful dance is from the Plains tradition and can be used to prepare yourself for deeper work in the spiritual realms. It helps you discover an important concept: you are the center of your universe.

The name of the dance is taken from the four mundane points of the compass: north, east, south, and west. Each direction has a certain property, a certain symbolism.

North: the place of old age, the night, winter, earth, green or black, a bear or buffalo

East: childhood, morning, springtime, air, white or yellow, an eagle or butterfly

South: adulthood, midday, summer, water, blue, a frog

West: middle age, evening, autumn, fire, red or orange, a thunderbird

Additionally, there are the directions up, representing the heavens or the Great Spirit; down, referring to the earth or the Divine Mother who nurtures us; and center, which is the center of our own being. To visualize this, you might imagine that you are at the center of a compass, suspended between heaven and earth. You are dancing in the heart of your universe, your feet anchored in the earth, with your head in the heavens, bringing in energy along the horizontal points of the compass, and pulling this energy into your own heart.

It is a powerful image. To tap into the power of the four directions, simply align yourself with a particular direction and ask it what you wish to know. Each of the directions has many values, many symbolisms, which vary according to different cultures and customs. We have suggested these symbols as a beginning.

THE DANCE OF THE FOUR DIRECTIONS

You will always be turning clockwise, or sunwise, as it is often called. Begin by facing whatever compass direction you wish to work with first. For this example, we'll start with the west. The starting position is a relaxed stance, with your feet about six inches apart.

During the dance, your feet will occupy an area about one-and-a-half feet square. One foot will always remain in its half of that small space as the other foot steps out to greet the proper direction in sequence. Your hands and eyes will draw in the energy of the direction as your foot returns to its starting position.

Your hands are pulling in the energy of the direction, bringing that energy into your heart. When you pull your hands in, cupped to hold the energy, bring your fingertips to your body until they touch the area of the thymus. The exact location is not critical; if you wish to measure, it is approximately two hand-widths below your thyroid gland (located in the voice-box area of your throat). As your hands touch your chest, follow them with your eyes to bring in even more energy. It may help to visualize a flowing light filling your hands, and in turn filling your heart.

Step 1: From the starting position, step forward to the west with your right foot as far as is comfortable. Keep your left foot stationary (although the left heel will lift

automatically as you step forward). When you step forward, push out with your hands from the level of your
heart, palms upward. As you bring your right foot back in
line with the left, the starting position, turn your softly
cupped hands back toward you and bring them back in to
touch your chest. As you do this, consciously feel the
energy you are drawing into your heart or Anahata.

Step 2: With your feet in the starting position, twist your
body a bit to your right and step out directly to the north
with your right foot. Push your hands out as before, from
the level of your heart, palms upward. As you bring your
right foot back in line with the left, bring the energy of the
north to your Anahata. Create the sensation of vitalizing
energy entering your chest area.

Step 3: From the starting position, twist your body slightly
to the left and step out directly to the south with your left
foot. Draw the energy from the south into your Anahata
as before.

Step 4: From the starting position, picking up your right
foot, twist your torso completely around, and step directly
behind you with the right foot so you are facing the east.
Your left foot remains in its starting position. Draw the
energy of the east to your Anahata with your hands as you
lift your right foot and twist back around to return to the
starting direction.

Step 5: From the starting position, draw energy from the
east by lifting your left foot and twisting your torso, this
time to the left so that you can step directly behind you.
Your right foot remains stationary this time. Draw in the
energy of the east to your Anahata as you move your left
foot and turn to place it back in the starting position.

Dance of the Four Directions

You have now completed one fourth of the dance, by addressing all directions from a starting position facing west. Now turn to your right and assume the starting position facing the north. Go through all five steps in sequence, drawing in energy from the north, then the east, then the west, and then steps 4 and 5 will be drawing energy from the south.

Continue by completing the five steps starting from the east, and then starting from the south. Always finish with the direction with which you began.

When you have ended the complete dance, thank each direction and the universe itself for sharing the energy with you.

This meditation can be experienced in silence or with a musical background. The speed of movement will vary according to your individual taste. If you wish to use a musical accompaniment, the most important thing will be to choose music with an even beat, and with a speed that feels comfortable to you. Frequently, this inner rhythm will change and the tempo of the meditation should then also change. Do not become so attached to a certain piece of music that you conform your inner rhythm to it rather than vice versa.

Part Two

THE EXERCISES

The exercises that follow are different forms of dynamic meditation. The logical, controlling left mode is given something it can do well: direct coordinated movement. When breath and all the elements of Part One are added to this physical structure, dynamic meditation results.

The first four systems — Red Dragon Chi Kung, T'ai Chi Chi Kung, T'ai Chi Ruler, and Earth Dancing — are explained in some detail, and each could comprise an entire exercise session for one day. The last three sections — Chakra Energizers, Indian Isometrics, and Yoga — should not be considered any less important than the others. This is especially true for Yoga, which is very complex and can become a way of life in itself. We have dealt with these last three more briefly because they are used in this book as specialized techniques for specific situations.

Red Dragon Chi Kung

The ancient Chinese Taoist alchemists were vitally concerned with health and longevity. They believed that if they could live long enough, they could achieve total spiritual realization. Their techniques built physical strength, but also spiritual strength. They believed that through their practices, they could build a "crystal body" (also called a spiritual body, or congealed soul) that would survive death, intact and aware. This enlightened soul would then lead to true immortality through the use of the techniques they had created. These Chinese Adepts are sometimes called the Taoist Immortals. Their techniques encompassed many elements of movement, meditation, breath, and diet.

Red Dragon Chi Kung is one system of exercise that is said to have been created by these Adepts. It consists of a series of movements using a long wooden or bamboo wand with copper caps on each end. This system was reserved for the elite for thousands of years. Death would have been the penalty for anyone else discovered practicing these arts.

On a subtle level, the dragon is a symbol of the dynamic energy in the body. On a physical level, it is symbolic of the cardiovascular system, where the bloodstream transports oxygen, carries away wastes, and defends the body against toxins and disease. Proper circulatory functioning is one of the keys to health and longevity.

Though these Red Dragon exercises work on the cardio-vascular system specifically, they benefit the body on all levels by opening energy meridians and by gently massaging the internal organs to keep them healthy and toned. Also, even though you will be surprised how these seemingly gentle exercises will quickly work you up into a sweat, they are much more gentle to your joints than jogging or conventional Western exercise programs. The pace can be as slow as you like, and at no time should you push yourself to the point of physical pain. Occasionally, try to stretch a bit more or add another nine repetitions, and you will make good progress.

As you perform the Red Dragon Chi Kung exercises, notice that when you are holding your wand with your hands at the ends and with your arms lowered, you are forming an upright triangle of energy with the apex at Sahasrara, the crown chakra. When you hold the wand overhead, an inverted triangle results, with the apex at Manipura, the power chakra. The wand itself collects and conducts energy through your palm chakras and up your arms to Sahasrara, or down your arms to Manipura. As the movements are performed, the wand helps circulate energy throughout the entire body.

We encourage performing the exercises in multiples of nine, after you've become accustomed to them physically. This is the Taoist esoteric number designed to maximize the benefits of the exercises. If you are stiff and out of shape or have other special physical difficulties, don't hesitate, however, to perhaps do three repetitions of any particular exercise at first, selecting the easier ones. Work up to nine repetitions and the more difficult movements gradually.

It is best to do these exercises to the accompaniment of dynamic music with an even beat. And of special note to women, because of the stimulation to your circulatory system, these exercises should not be performed while you are pregnant or menstruating.

Making Your Own Long Wand

To get a wand of the proper length, find something with which to experiment, like a length of plastic pipe or a long broom handle. With your improvised wand over your head, hold one end and estimate where your other hand would comfortably be to hold the other end. Adjust the distance between your hands so there will be about four inches between your head and the wand. Mark that spot and measure the length carefully.

We have constructed our wands from 1¼-inch wooden doweling, which can be obtained at a building supply or hardware store. Pine will be the cheapest and most commonly found. We have also used oak and ash, which are a little bit more expensive, but also inherently more magical. Have your chosen doweling cut to the correct length. Buy two copper caps (found in the plumbing section of the same store) to slip snugly over the ends of the wand. You may need to sand the wand ends a bit before they will accept the caps. These copper caps help collect and conduct the energy generated as you exercise.

Placing small magnets inside the copper caps before placing them on the wand seems to amplify the energy created. You also might try experimenting with various gemstone crystals. Try placing a small, perfect Herkimer diamond (a type of double terminated quartz crystal) beneath each copper cap.

The wooden wand can be finished according to personal taste. You may want to retain the natural wood finish, or apply paint and wipe it off while it is still wet to give the effect of colored stain. Spray paint can be used to apply colored opaque bands, using metallic silver and gold for accents.

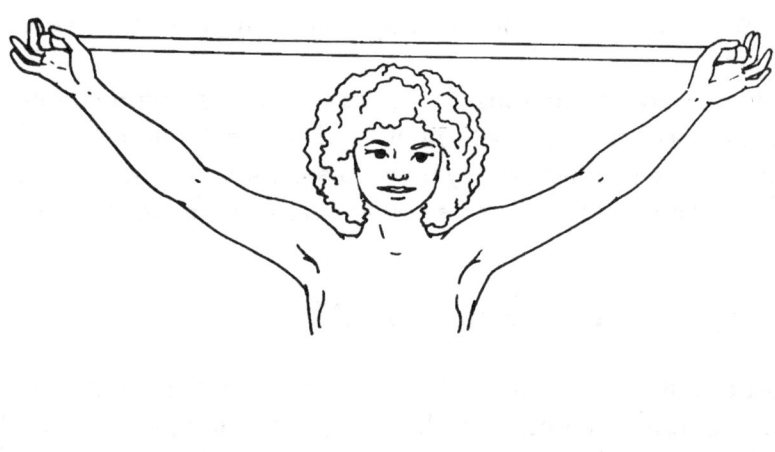

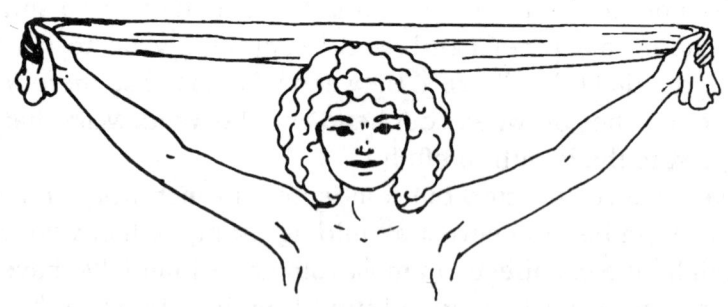

Tools for Red Dragon Chi Kung

It is certainly acceptable to create a wand out of bamboo, which is traditional, or even a piece of rigid plastic pipe, simple and unadorned, which one of our students preferred. Instead of a wand, it is also possible to use a cloth held tautly between your outstretched arms. Do be aware that this technique, however, puts a different emphasis on the movements and different tensions on the arms and back, and is not traditional.

Above all, be flexible and remember your preferences and needs may change as you progress in your self-discovery.

Red Dragon Chi Kung Basic Technique

The beginning stance for Red Dragon Chi Kung is a poised posture, with feet about six inches apart, and both hands centered on the wand which is held at the level of Manipura. Your back should be straight, pelvis relaxed, elbows relaxed, and knees slightly bent. Never lock the knees or elbows, as this restricts the circulation of chi and body fluids.

In some standing movements, the feet remain together; in others, a wider stance is required. To achieve the wide stance, gracefully slide the right foot out to the correct position. This should be completed in one flowing motion. At the completion of each set of standing exercises, return to the beginning stance, with the wand at the level of Manipura. Stand quietly for a few moments, breathing normally, before going to the next set of exercises. You should perform the exercises in the order given: standing exercises first, then moving to the floor. In between sets for the exercises on the floor, pause for a few moments in whatever position you ended the exercise before continuing.

During the pauses between sets, you may either empty your mind or use this time for visualization techniques to aid the flow of energy. As you rest, you may also reestablish the upright and inverted triangles either by raising or lowering your wand to refocus your mind and your energies, if you feel the need.

In most cases, we have given directions for one repetition of the exercise. Continue in the same manner for 9, 18, or 36 repetitions to make a complete set.

DRAGON BREATH

This technique prepares you for Red Dragon Chi Kung exercises.

Sit cross-legged on the ground. Reach between your crossed legs and grasp your feet, fingers on top, thumbs underneath on your soles. Press your thumbs firmly into the soles of your feet, just where your arch starts, under the ball of your foot. You should locate a tender area. This is "Bubbling Spring," the chakra where you can pull energy up or push it down. Maintain a constant probing pressure with your thumbs on this point throughout the exercise.

Inhale slowly 20 times through your nose. At the last inhalation, hold your breath as long as you comfortably can.

Stick your tongue out and pant, inhaling and exhaling rapidly 20 times.

At the final panting breath, hold your breath as long as you comfortably can.

Exhale with the dragon sound "Hing." Let the final "ng" of this word continue to ring inside your head, like a hum, so that you feel the vibration up in your crown chakra at Sahasrara. Then relax.

You may repeat this sequence several times, but no more than nine times.

Charging your body with life force,
drawn in on your breath.

Dragon Breath

PYRAMID POWER

Technique

> From the beginning stance, slide your right foot out until your feet are shoulder width apart, and move your hands out to the ends of the wand. This establishes the basic upright triangle shape.
>
> Inhale. Bring your wand straight over your head, establishing the inverted triangle.
>
> Exhale. Lower your wand behind you to the small of your back, creating another triangle behind you.
>
> Inhale. Raise your wand overhead to create the fourth triangle.

Inner Space

Feel that you are building a pyramid of energy around your body. See this pyramid with your inner eye.

Pyramid Power

SNAKE TWISTING

This exercise trims and firms your waist and increases spinal flexibility.

Technique

> With feet together, slide your hands out to the ends of the wand. Raise the wand overhead and then lower it behind your head to rest on top of your shoulders.
>
> Inhale, twist to your right, and then face forward.
>
> Exhale, twist to your left, and then face forward.

Inner Space

This exercise balances the left and right sides of your brain. Be conscious of the centering effect, and that you are at the pivoting center. The sinuous twisting and flexing places you in the realm of the snake, whose coiling is a powerful source of stored energy, waiting to be released.

Snake Twisting

GREETING THE SUN

Technique

Stand with your feet together and slide your hands out to the ends of the wand. Raise the wand overhead and then lower it behind your head to the top of your shoulders.

Inhale and arch backward slightly, tipping your chin up so you feel a nice stretch between the tip of your chin and your pubic bone.

Exhale and bend over forward as far as you can, while still keeping your back straight. The wand remains behind your shoulders.

Inner Space

If you are outdoors, especially at sunrise, this is a lovely exercise. As you bend and straighten, try to feel the warmth on your chest. Greet the sun and the new day, filling yourself with life force, vibrant and strong, ready for adventures and challenges the day might bring.

The exercise can be just as energizing when indoors, because you can recreate the warmth of the rising sun in your inner eye, feel it, and draw strength from it, no matter what the time of day, or where you are.

Greeting the Sun

DRAGON'S TAIL TWITCHES

Technique

The speed of the exercise will be governed by the time it takes you to comfortably and completely inhale and exhale. For this reason, do not rush the movements. This exercise gently massages most of the internal organs, and helps the spine and back muscles.

> From the beginning stance, slide your right foot out to a medium stance and move your hands to the ends of the wand. Raise the wand overhead and lower it behind your head to rest on top of your shoulders. Inhale.

> Exhale and twist to the right, looking in that direction and swinging the left end of the wand across in front of you.

> Inhale as you return to the center position.

> Exhale as you tilt your torso sideways in the same direction, the right end of the wand swinging down to almost touch the right side of your body. Then inhale as you return to the center position.

> Exhale as you twist to the left, looking in that direction and swinging the right end of the wand across in front of you. Then inhale as you return to the center position.

> Exhale as you tilt your torso sideways in the same direction, the left end of the wand swinging down to almost touch the left side of your body. Then inhale as you return to the center position.

Inner Space

Imagine yourself as the dragon twisting, turning, bending. Feel yourself flow into this exercise as vital energy spirals throughout your body, charging your being with cosmic life force.

Dragon's Tail Twitches

DRAGON ON A TIGHTROPE

Try to achieve a deeper knee bend each time you go down. This somewhat difficult balancing movement creates strength and grace in your whole being.

Technique

> Slide your right foot out to as wide a stance as you find comfortable, while simultaneously sliding your hands out to the ends of the wand. Turn your feet so your toes are pointing out, as if you are walking a tightrope. Raise your wand overhead and gracefully lower it to rest behind your head on top of your shoulders.
>
> Inhale.
>
> Exhale as you bend your knees and squat down a few inches, keeping your back straight as though you are sliding down a wall.
>
> Inhale as you return to the upright position.

Inner Space

To accomplish this movement successfully, see yourself as confident, energized, and centered without fear. Be securely balanced on the tightrope, with your chest held proudly up, your back straight, and your determination unwavering.

Dragon on a Tightrope

INFINITY

After doing 9, 18, or 36 repetitions on the right side, change so that you lower your left arm until the wand is roughly parallel to your left side. Then bring the wand down behind you and continue the exercise for the same number of repetitions as you did when starting from the right. After working in both directions, you will have completed one set. Try to pick up speed as you gain coordination.

Technique

> Breathe normally as you do this movement. Move your right foot out until your feet are shoulder width apart, slipping your hands out to the ends of the wand as you do so.
>
> Raise the wand above your head, establishing an inverted triangle.
>
> Lower your right arm until the wand is roughly parallel to your right side. This automatically brings your left hand to a position above your head.
>
> Bring the wand back by lowering your left hand. This establishes an upright triangle behind you.
>
> Raise your right arm until your right hand is above your head and your left hand remains at your left side. The wand will now be parallel to your left side.
>
> Bring the wand forward and down in front of your body by lowering your right hand, establishing an upright triangle in front of you.

Inner Space

You are weaving a pyramid of energy around yourself at the same time that your wand ends are describing a figure eight or infinity symbol. Try to remain peaceful within the center of this energy.

Infinity

DRAGON TWISTING

Technique

This exercise will create suppleness in your torso.

> From the beginning stance, slide out your right foot while slipping your hands to the ends of the wand.
>
> Inhale and raise your wand to beneath your chin.
>
> Exhale and bend over, reaching toward your toes with the wand. Keep your back as straight as possible.
>
> Inhale as you return to the upright position.
>
> Exhale as you twist to your right and bend over, reaching toward the side of your right foot with the wand.
>
> Inhale as you straighten and twist forward.
>
> Exhale as you twist to your left and bend over, reaching toward the side of the left foot with the wand.
>
> Inhale as you straighten and twist forward.

Inner Space

You are drawing chi up your body's meridians and then pulling it down. Feel the energy twisting and coiling within as you bend and turn.

Dragon Twisting

DRAGON LUNGING

Technique

Breathe normally as you do this movement. Start with your feet side by side.

Slide your hands about eight inches apart on the wand, which is held at the level of Manipura.

Step forward vigorously with your right foot as though lunging. As you do this, thrust the wand forward in an arching motion.

Return your right foot to the beginning stance. Bring the wand back in, scooping it downward and then pulling it back to the level of Manipura as you bring your foot back. The ends of the wand will have just made an ellipse.

Lunge out now with your left foot, thrusting the wand forward simultaneously in the same manner as before. Return to the beginning stance.

Inner Space

This exercise is vigorous, dynamic and challenging to perform. You are a dragon lunging, full of infinite strength and vitality.

Dragon Lunging

DRAGON BOWING

Technique

From the beginning stance, with feet together, release your left hand from the wand, gracefully slip the wand behind your back, and grasp it again with your left hand. Experiment with hand spacing on the wand for this exercise. Some people hold the wand at the ends, while others prefer to hold their hands closer together.

Inhale and arch backward until you feel a firm stretch between your chin and your pubic bone. The wand will naturally drop behind you as you arch.

Exhale and bend forward at the waist as far as you can comfortably go, keeping your back straight and lifting the wand as straight up as you can. Be careful not to lift too far forward with your arms.

Inhale as you return to the upright position, in preparation for arching back again.

Inner Space

This is a beautifully exhilarating exercise that sends energy flowing through you from the crown of your head to the soles of your feet. Try to "see" and feel this rush of vital life force energizing your body.

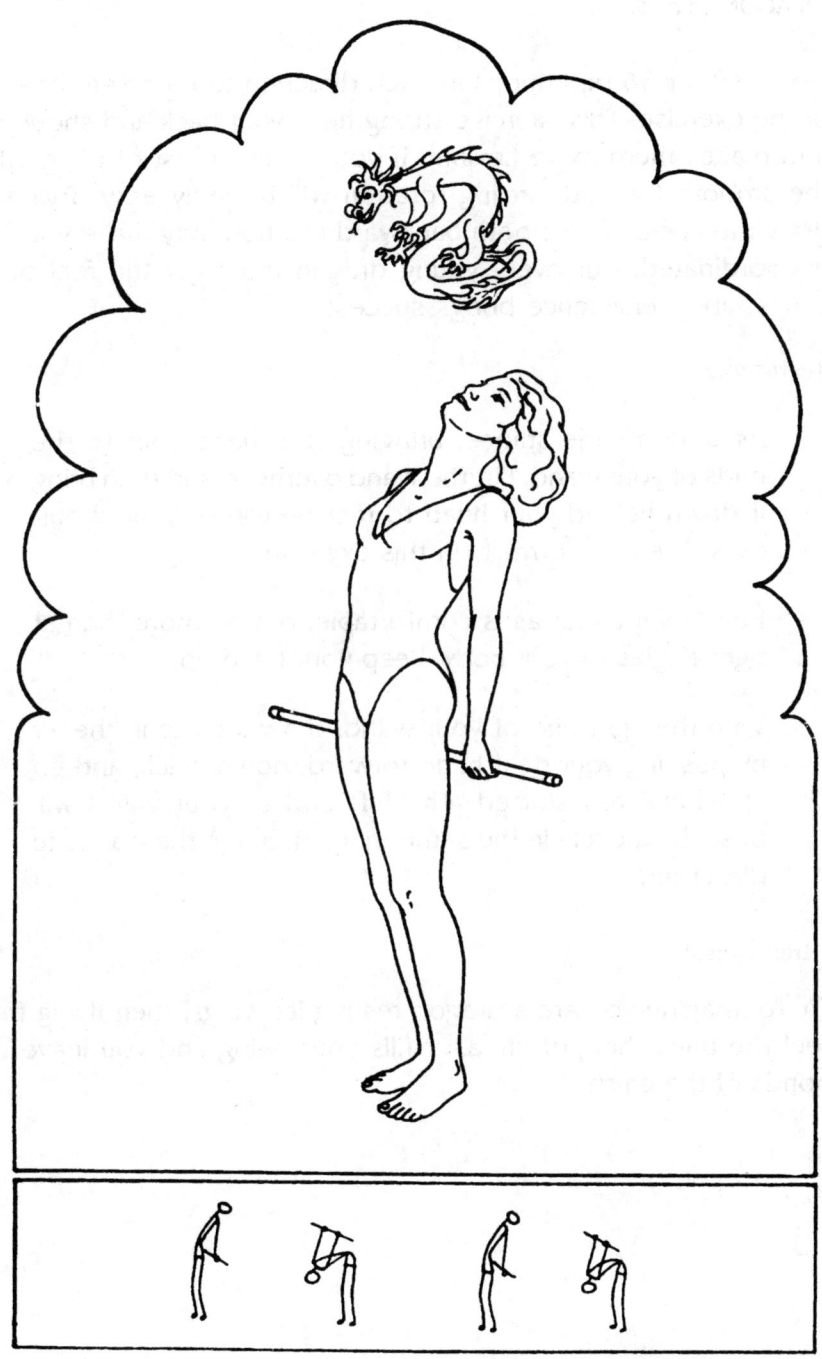

Dragon Bowing

DRAGON FLYING

Do 9, 18, or 36 repetitions in each direction to complete one set of the exercise. This exercise strengthens your back and shoulders and makes them more flexible. If you are like most of us, getting the smooth forward circling rotation will be fairly easy. Trying to draw the circle in a smooth backward rotation may make you feel uncoordinated. But every young dragon must get the feel of its wings, and persistence brings success.

Technique

Assume a wide stance, bringing your hands out to the ends of your wand. Lift the wand overhead and then bring it down behind your head to rest on top of your shoulders. Breathe normally in this exercise.

Bend over as far as is comfortable, but no more than at right angles to your body. Keep your head up.

With the right end of your wand, draw a circle in the air by pushing your right hand forward, down, back, and up to where you started. The left end of your wand will describe a circle in the same manner, but in the opposite direction.

Inner Space

Try to imagine you are a dragon testing its wings, then flying free. Feel the unleashing of chi as it fills your being and you leave the bonds of the earth.

Dragon Flying

CRANE FOLDING ITS WINGS

Be gentle as you roll the wand up your neck; the muscles may be tender. Let the downward pressure on the wand increase as you massage the tense muscles.

Technique

Slide your right foot out to a wide stance, while simultaneously sliding your hands out to the ends of the wand. Raise the wand overhead, then lower it smoothly behind your head to rest on top of your shoulders. Do not hold the wand with your hands, but rather lay your wrists on top of the wand at each end.

Inhale.

Exhale as you bend forward with your back straight, letting the wand roll a little up the back of your neck. As you do this, let the wand roll from under your wrists to under your elbows. At the extreme forward bend, the wand will rest at the base of your skull and your arms will be hanging down over the wand.

Inhale as you return to the upright position.

Inner Space

This movement brings energy up your spine, infusing your brain with vital pranic energy, helping you to be both refreshed and centered.

Crane Folding Its Wings

CRANE OPENS TO HEAVEN

Keep an even pace, trying to bend your knees farther as you progress.

Technique

> Slide your right foot out to a wide stance, while simultaneously sliding your hands out to the ends of the wand.
>
> Inhale and raise your wand straight overhead.
>
> Exhale and lower the wand behind your body to your lower back, doing as deep a knee bend as possible as you do so. Try not to pull your knees together as you squat down. To help keep your back straight, imagine you are sliding down a wall; don't lean forward.
>
> Inhale and return to the upright position.

Inner Space

You are a great bird, opening your wings to the sky, momentarily expansive and vulnerable as you crouch in readiness to take flight. Remember that there is great strength in vulnerability.

Crane Opens to Heaven

DRAGON SHOULDER SHRUGS

After 9, 18, or 36 repetitions in one direction, reverse the rotation of your shoulders and do the same number of repetitions in the other direction. You are describing a smooth circle with the point of each shoulder, drawing the top half as you inhale, and the bottom half as you exhale. Always end the standing portion of Red Dragon Chi Kung with this exercise, to release any tension in your shoulders.

Technique

> Stand with feet together, holding the wand at the level of Manipura. Releasing your right hand, slide the wand behind you and grip it again with your right hand. Your arms lie alongside your body and your hands, grasping the wand well in from the ends, will be alongside your hips.
>
> Inhale as you rotate your shoulders up and back.
>
> Exhale as you rotate your shoulders down and forward.

Inner Space

Feel the tension as you rotate your shoulders. As you reach the bottom part of the rotation, let the tension go out of your body.

Dragon Shoulder Shrugs

DRAGON WALK

Technique

Sit on the floor, your back straight, with your legs together and resting straight in front of you.

Raise your wand overhead, establishing an inverted triangle, then lower it behind your head to rest on your shoulders. Hold the wand at each end.

Inhale and "walk" forward on your buttocks, with your right side going forward first. Advance three steps, twisting your torso first to the left, then the right, and then the left again in coordination with your forward movement. Try to twist far enough so that the wand is in line with your legs each time.

Exhale as you "walk" three steps back to your original position, twisting each time in the same manner.

Inner Space

This is an exercise in self esteem. Visualize you are a strong, vibrant dragon. The movement might feel clumsy at first — perhaps you are a young, inexperienced dragon — but do not allow your bright image to fade.

Dragon Walk

DRAGON TOUCHES TOES

Technique

Sit on the floor with your back straight. Smoothly sweep your legs out as wide as you can comfortably manage, bringing your hands out to the ends of the wand as you do so.

Inhale and raise the wand straight above your head, establishing the inverted pyramid.

Exhale and twist your torso so the wand is aligned with your right leg, and lower the right end of the wand to your right foot.

Inhale and return to the upright center position.

Exhale and twist your torso so the wand is aligned with your left leg and lower the left end of the wand to your left foot.

Inhale and return to the upright center position.

Inner Space

Each time you are upright, you are inhaling chi energy into your solar plexus or Manipura. Each time you exhale and touch your toes, you are sending bright chi energy down the side of your body you are leaning toward.

Dragon Touches Toes

DRAGON ROWING (FEET TOGETHER)

Vigorously row with the wand, as if you were holding the ends of a pair of long oars. Go up and forward with the wand, and then lean back as you complete the "stroke" to get the maximum effect of this exercise. It will strengthen your torso, firming your stomach muscles especially.

Technique

Sit on the floor with your knees drawn up and your back straight. Bring your legs firmly together. Slide your hands out to the ends of the wand, which is held in front of you.

Inhale and bring the wand up beneath your chin as you lean back as far as you can without losing your balance.

Exhale and smoothly lean forward, pushing the wand well up and over your knees toward your feet in an arching motion.

Inhale and lean backward again as you pull the wand back, up and over your knees, drawing it down close to your body as you bring it back almost to your chin.

Inner Space

Try to imagine you are actually rowing a boat through a sea of bright energy. Vibrant life force collects by your oars, and as you move steadily back and forth, you are bathing your entire body with chi.

Dragon Rowing (Feet Together)

DRAGON ROWING (FEET APART)

Other than having your feet spread apart, the directions are the same as for the other Dragon Rowing exercise. You must still row vigorously as if you are holding a pair of oars, arching as far up and forward as you can, and then stroking back as far as possible. The tension on your legs will be different, however, and you will bend further forward at the waist, creating more of a stretch on your spine.

Technique

Sit on the floor with your knees drawn up and your back straight. Slide your feet out to about three feet apart. At the same time, bring your hands out to the ends of the wand, which is held in front of you.

Inhale and bring the wand up beneath your chin as you lean back as far as you can without losing your balance.

Exhale and smoothly lean forward, pushing the wand well up and over your knees and down toward your toes in an arching motion.

Inhale and lean backward as you pull the wand back, up and over your knees, drawing it down close to your body as you bring it back almost to your chin.

Inner Space

With your legs apart and braced against the sides of an imaginary boat, this exercise asks that you dig a little deeper, pull a little harder on the oars, and create a slightly more powerful flow of chi up your spine and up your wand.

Dragon Rowing (Feet Apart)

DRAGON SIDE THRUSTS

If you are in average condition, you may not be able to do much more than bring the tip of the wand to a spot somewhere between your feet.

Technique

From a sitting position on the floor or ground, slide your feet apart as wide as is comfortable, while simultaneously slipping your hands out to the tips of the wand. Raise the wand overhead and then lower it behind your head until it rests on top of your shoulders.

Inhale.

Exhale, and twisting your body to your right, attempt to touch your right foot with your left hand which is holding the end of the wand. Do not allow the wand to slide very much on your shoulder, or allow your legs to move.

Inhale as you return to the starting position.

Exhale and repeat the movement on your other side.

Inner Space

One woman said her inner space for this exercise was something like "Dragon being tortured." She was very stiff in her torso at the start, but as time passed she became increasingly more flexible. Keep positive energy in your mind for this most difficult posture.

Dragon Side Thrusts

DRAGON ROLLING

After practice, some people can roll backward until their toes go over and touch the floor behind their head, and then smoothly roll forward until their head touches the floor in front to complete the maximum roll possible. Others, like one elderly person we know, could only rock a little on their buttocks. Do what you can and you will probably discover your capacity increasing as your body tones itself.

Technique

Sit on the floor with your knees drawn up, and ankles together. Lay the wand across the tops of your ankles. Slip your hands down between your legs, then under them to the outside of your ankles where you grasp the wand. Position your hands close to your ankles. Breathe normally throughout the exercise.

Roll backward as far as you comfortably can. Watch your head and neck and do not roll too far back at first.

Throw yourself forward again and roll as far as you can.

Inner Space

Be conscious of the energy generated along your spine as you roll against Mother Earth (remember that she is always there, under the floor somewhere).

Dragon Rolling

Dragon Points to Heaven

After you have done 9, 18, or 36 repetitions on one side, move to the other side and repeat the exercise the same number of times to complete one set. This exercise will probably be difficult at first. Resist the inclination to roll your hips back to make it easier; they should remain snugly against the wand at all times. If you persist in trying to do the movement correctly, you will find your hip joints becoming much more flexible.

Technique

> Lay down on your left side. Hold the wand upright with one end on the ground next to your body. Your left hand holds the wand on the floor, and your right hand is about one third of the way up.

> Inhale and bring your right leg up as close to the wand as possible, toe pointed to heaven, leg straight. Hold this position a few moments.

> Exhale as you lower your straight leg down to the starting position.

Inner Space

As you sweep your toe heavenward, imagine sparkling chi being swept upward also, until at the apex, your toe is pointing at the stars, in direct communication with them.

Dragon Points to Heaven

DRAGON STRETCHES

This is a strenuous exercise. Try to lift gracefully, without jerking.

Technique

> Lie face down on the floor with your wand resting in front of you, at right angles to your body. Grasp the wand with your hands, about shoulder width apart.
>
> Inhale as you raise your head up and look up, arching your back. At the same time, raise your straight right leg (toe pointed) as high as you can.
>
> Exhale, lowering your leg and your head simultaneously.
>
> Inhale and repeat the movement with your left leg.

Inner Space

Visualize that you are a beautiful dragon stretching luxuriously, first one side and then the other. Feel the tingling and energizing stretch from your chin to the tip of your toes (claws?).

Dragon Stretches

BALANCE OF THE FIVE ELEMENTS

Technique

Slide out to a wide stance, simultaneously moving your hands out to the ends of the wand. Raise the wand overhead and lower it behind you to the top of your shoulders, where it remains throughout the exercise.

Inhale and arch your body and head back slightly, looking upward as you do so, feeling a stretch between your chin and your pubic bone.

Exhale as you straighten and then lean forward a little, head still lifted, eyes looking upward. Say "earth" as you lean forward. Inhale and arch backwards as before.

Exhale as you straighten and lean foward again, this time bending forward a little more than before, head lifted, eyes looking upward. Say "water" as you lean forward. Inhale and arch as before.

Continue in this same manner, saying next "fire," then "air," and then "ether." Lean farther forward as you name each element, until for ether, you are leaning as far forward as is comfortable, while still maintaining a slight stretch between your chin and your pubic bone by arching your back.

Inhale after you have leaned forward to say "ether," and return to an upright position.

Inner Space

In this exercise, through movement, breath, and the recitation of the names of the traditional elements, you are creating a flow of energy up your spine. First, you pull energy to your base chakra, then higher each time, until you are pulling the energy to your crown as you say "ether." Visualize the flow and you will feel it.

Balance of the Five Elements

T'ai Chi Chi Kung

The T'ai Chi Chi Kung movements presented here, like those of Red Dragon Chi Kung, were devised by the ancient Chinese Immortals to help achieve health and long life. Originally, they were probably a martial arts form, but were later adapted to become a rejuvenation system.

These movements are energy generators. They build and move chi, or pranic energy, along the body's meridians, much the same way as the Red Dragon exercises do, but without the use of a wand.

These fluid and graceful movements help build strength and balance, both physically and mentally. Since the energy meridians correspond to the nervous system on a physical level, T'ai Chi Chi Kung will improve the health of your nervous system and certain glandular and lymphatic functions.

T'ai Chi Chi Kung Basic Technique

For the beginning stance for all the exercises, stand with your back straight, pelvis relaxed, arms at your sides with your elbows slightly bent, and with your feet together and your knees slightly bent. Always slide out with your right foot first, if a wider stance is required.

As you do the movements, maintain a focus on Manipura. Imagine a golden sun radiating life force energy at your solar plexus.

In some of the movements, you will observe that your hands circle above your head and then move down the center line of your body, down past your Manipura to your sides. Your left hand should be closest to your body, palm inward. Your right hand will be just behind the left, palm also inward, never touching, which would affect the flow of chi you are generating. Always perform this hand movement in the same way whenever it appears in the exercises. It is very important never to touch the hands together or against the body as this short-circuits the flow of chi through the body.

As you perform T'ai Chi Chi Kung, remember always: you are not just a collection of flesh, blood, and bones, doing a physical routine. You are a Being of Light who hopes to make your Body of Light even more vibrant with physical and spiritual life force.

When you move your body, chi energy moves with you; an intangible, invisible, but very real energy force. As you continue performing these exercises over a period of time, you will become attuned to this energy force and will come to a space where you will actually be able to feel it as a physical sensation flowing along your body's meridians.

Some people who are very familiar with this system like to choreograph a graceful dance, flowing from one exercise to another, stepping forward and back in a fluid energy dance. The music will depend on the speed of execution of the individual exercises. A rhythmic beat is best. Don't be rigid. Learn the exercises and then don't be afraid to vary the technique as you listen to your inner feelings.

As with the previous exercises, do 9, 18, or 36 repetitions for a complete set unless otherwise instructed.

AWAKENING CHI

Here is the technique for preliminary breathing prior to T'ai Chi Chi Kung (also for T'ai Chi Ruler):

> Slide your right foot out until your feet are shoulder width apart. Your feet are turned slightly inward; your knees are slightly bent. Gaze forward as you do the exercises, to help maintain your inward focus.
>
> Rest your hands on the top of your thighs. Inhale as you assume Moola bandha, then exhale and relax Moola bandha. As you inhale each time, your stomach will expand; as you exhale, it will contract. This is called breathing to your stomach. Repeat ten times.
>
> Bring your arms straight up in front of you, elbows slightly flexed, with your palms facing outward. Breathe in and out of your chest, so that it expands and contracts, which is called breathing to your chest. Do not maintain Moola bandha. Breathe in and out ten times.
>
> Bring your arms up straight out from your sides, as high as your shoulders. Your palms face outward. Breathe in and out into your chest, without Moola bandha, ten times.
>
> Bring your arms forward about 18 inches or so and drop them down about waist high, with palms facing outward. Inhale and exhale into your stomach, maintaining and relaxing Moola bandha with each breath. Repeat ten times.

This technique generates and circulates chi energy in a powerful way, preparing your body for the movements to follow.

Awakening Chi

GATHERING CHI

Technique

In this exercise, each of your hands is a mirror image of the other. Draw your hands up from your sides, then reach outward and to the side with your hands open, palms away from you, and scoop a large circle of energy in toward your body. Your hands will each "draw" a complete large circle and end up "holding" a ball of energy. Then, you will turn your palms over and push the excess energy straight down to Mother Earth.

> Inhale. From the beginning stance, slide your right foot out and simultaneously scoop up a ball of energy with both hands, as described above.

> Exhale. Turn your hands over, palms down, and press your palms down toward the ground, returning the energy you have gathered and do not need.

> This completes the movement. You may gather chi three times if you wish, returning the excess energy to Mother Earth each time. Generally, it is done preceding your T'ai Chi Chi Kung session, and periodically during the session after about every five sets of exercises.

Inner Space

It is especially helpful to perform this exercise barefoot so you can more easily feel the energy being pulled and gathered up through your body meridians into Manipura. You are also scooping up energy with your hands, of course, where the chi force flows in through your Lao Kun of each hand, following the meridians to your Manipura. As you scoop with your hands, try to visualize clearly the flow of energy as you gather it, circulate it, and return some of it to earth. In time, you will be able to actually feel this flow.

Gathering Chi

CRANE BALANCING DRAGON

Technique

With your feet together, form the "Cranes' Beaks" with your hands, fingers touching your shoulders. Breathe naturally.

Raise your right hand, turning your head to look up toward it. At the same time, lift your left leg, bending it at the knee.

Do the same thing on the other side, raising your left hand and turning your head to look upward at it, as you lift your right leg.

Alternate this sequence, slowly at first, and then building up speed as you become more coordinated. Repeat as many times as you wish.

Inner Space

The brain is in halves, the intuitive and the logical, the right and left modes. In metaphysical language, it is referred to as yin and yang, female and male. In most people, these separate hemispheres generally function alternatively, with one side or the other dominant. This exercise doesn't look too complicated, but if you are very dominant on one side of your brain, and therefore physically "lopsided," this exercise can be difficult. It helps to integrate the mechanics of the left and right modes, promoting a balance, a centering. Imagine yourself achieving this perfect balance, in which your brain is at peace with itself, resting from its ceaseless tug of war.

Crane Balancing Dragon

CRANE SPREADS WINGS

As in any leaning over position, do not rush this exercise, or you may become light-headed.

Technique

> Slide your feet out to a wide stance. Inhale and sweep your arms up until your hands are overhead, with your palms up.
>
> Still holding your "wing tips" overhead, rotate your wrists so that your palms are facing down, and form "Cranes' Beaks" by holding your fingers and thumbs together.
>
> Exhale as you squat slightly, and leaning over, sweep your arms up and back behind you, still holding the "Cranes' Beaks" hand position.
>
> Release the "Cranes' Beaks" and now cup your hands.
>
> Inhale as you scoop your cupped hands forward and up, lifting your torso, returning to your upright position with your "wing tips" overhead, hands palm up, in preparation for the next repetition.

Inner Space

This somewhat complicated movement is an energizing, full-body workout. Take your time and understand all parts of the bird symbolism and the gathering of energy as you stand back upright. You bow, you gather energy, then stretch upward and spread your wings, as if testing the air before flight.

Crane Spreads Wings

CRANE ABOUT TO FLY

Technique

Your feet remain together as you stand relaxed, with your
hands at your sides.

Inhale and rise on your toes. Bring your hands above your
head and press your palms together firmly.

Hold this pose for a few seconds, balancing on your toes,
pressing your hands together, and holding your breath.
Then rotate your wrists outward, so that your palms face
away from each other.

Exhale and return your heels to the ground as you gracefully glide your arms down on each side of your body. Let
your hands smoothly continue toward each other, where
they almost meet at the center line of your body. Do not
touch your hands together, as this will short-circuit the
energy flow. Just hold them one over the other, slightly
cupped, about an inch or so apart. Your slightly cupped
hands pause there, in preparation for the next repetition.

Inner Space

As you rise on your toes and press your hands together (which creates an isometric tension), you are building chi. As you relax and
release the tension, you will experience a rush of chi energy flowing
through your body. In this exercise you are a beautiful bird that is
just about to spring into the air and fly. Feel the wind (energy) in
your face.

Crane about to Fly

CRANE IN FLIGHT

Technique

Take a wide stance, and press your palms together in front of your center line.

Inhale as you rise on your toes and sweep your arms out and upward, as if unfurling your wings. If you have difficulty keeping your balance, try focusing on a spot in front of you at eye level.

Draw your hands together again, palms touching.

Exhale as you lean forward at the waist, lower your heels to the floor, and swing your hands (palms still pressed together) down between your legs.

Return to the upright position, flat-footed, with your palms pressed together. Prepare to inhale as you begin again.

Inner Space

You are a great bird in flight, your wings folding and opening again in powerful strokes as you rise into the freedom of flight.

Crane in Flight

ROCKING CRANE

Technique

Slide your right foot forward; keep your hands at your sides. Inhale and sweep your arms up in front of you. Arch your hands up to your chin. Your wrists are relaxed; let your hands trail with fingers down as you circle your hands back up to your chin. As you sweep your arms forward, your left heel will lift off the floor and your right foot will be flat on the ground. As you circle your hands to your chin, your weight shifts back and your left heel will drop.

Exhale as you arch your hands away from your chin, palms forward, in a reverse of the previous motion. When your arms complete the circular motion and are fully extended downward, relax your wrists for the next repetition. Shift back and forth on your feet to create the rocking motion.

Repeat these steps for 9, 18, or 36 repetitions. Then reverse the sequence in the following manner.

Start with your hands, palms facing away, in front of your chin. Inhale normally. Exhale as you arch your hands away from your chin, circling them down to your sides, rocking forward and back on your feet as before. Inhale and circle your hands back up to your chin as before, with the same rocking motion.

Repeat these last steps for the same number of repetitions as for the first. Then do the entire sequence with the left foot forward, to complete one set of this exercise.

Inner Space

You are pulling chi into your body and circulating the energy down to your Manipura. Try to be conscious of the image of this bright energy flowing into your hands, up your arms, and down to your power chakra.

Rocking Crane

TURNING THE WHEEL OF THE LAW

Technique

Lift your right foot at the heel and slide it out in front of you. Turn your left foot out at a 45-degree angle to your right foot, so you can shift freely with the motion of your hands. Bend your arms at the elbows, as if you were holding a tray, except that your palms must be facing downward. Your hands will be about one foot apart.

With your hands starting in close to your body, inhale as you circle your hands to the left and "draw" the left side of the circle. Twist your body to the left.

Exhale as you continue around the circle, twisting to your right, ending with your hands in front of your body again. Twist your body to the left, then to the right, and shift your weight as necessary to follow the circular motion all the way around and remain securely balanced.

Do 9, 18, or 36 circles in this direction. Then, reverse your hands to a palms up position and do the same number of repetitions. This completes half a set of this exercise.

Now, step back to the beginning stance and then slide your left foot out and repeat the entire sequence palms down, and then palms up. Use the same number of repetitions, whether 9, 18, or 36, to remain balanced throughout. This will complete one set of this exercise.

Inner Space

Energy projects from your Lao Kun (palm chakras). As you circle your hands palms down, you are connecting with the energy force of Mother Earth. As you circle your hands palms up, you are connecting with Father Sky. Try to be aware of this connection — it is intimate and real, and will help charge you with life force energy.

Turning the Wheel of the Law

HOLDING UP THE HEAVENS

This movement creates isometric tension in your arms and body. Keeping your arms snugly against your body massages the lymph glands under your arms particularly.

Technique

Stand relaxed with your feet together, and hands at your sides.

Inhale and lock your fingers together, keeping your upper arms snugly against your body. Bring your locked hands, palms up, beneath your chin. Then turn your locked hands so that your palms are facing down, and continue to bring your hands up to the level of the crown of your head. Turn them over to a palms up position. Straighten your arms upward as you continue to stretch as far as you can. Keep your hands locked until, at the extreme of your reach, you release your locked fingers.

Exhale, letting your hands separate and sweep smoothly down and out to your sides (palms down). Then bring them up to the center line of your body, where you again lock your fingers, palms up, in preparation for the next repetition.

Inner Space

As you release your hands and sweep your arms back down, the tension in your body releases and you receive a rush of oxygen and chi. Imagine you are thirstily drawing golden chi energy up through your chakras, past Sahasrara at your crown. Then, when you sweep your arms back down, you shower yourself with pulsating light.

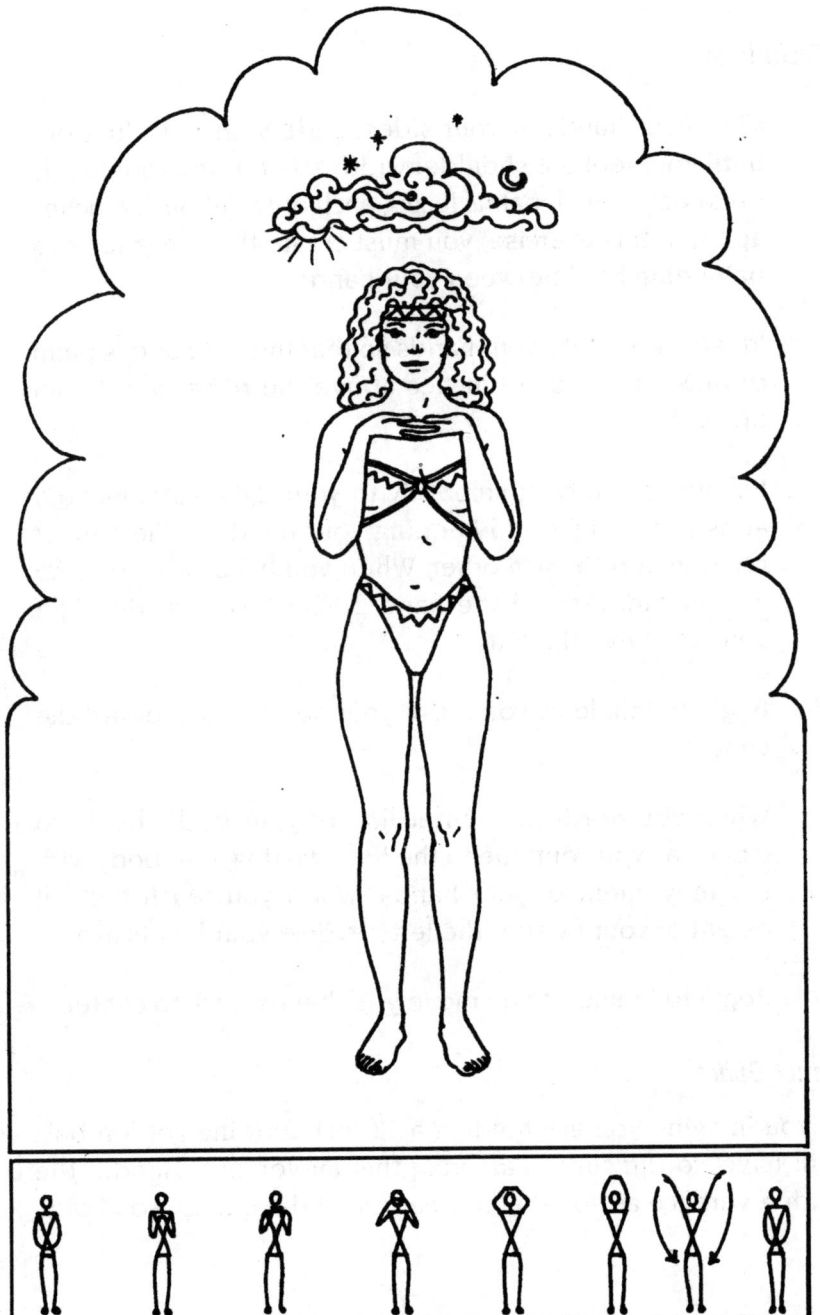

Holding Up the Heavens

PROJECTING LIGHT

Technique

With your hands at your sides, slide your right foot out until your feet are shoulder width apart. Bring your hands up to waist level, palms facing each other, about 12 inches apart. In this exercise, you must create the sensation of a ball being held between your hands.

Inhale and rotate your hands so that the left hand is palm downward, about 12 inches above the right hand (palm upward).

Exhale as you twist smoothly to your right, rotating your arms to the right and keeping your hands in the correct relationship to each other. When you have twisted as far as you can, reverse the hand position so that the right hand is above the left.

Begin to inhale as you move your hands back toward the center.

When you reach the center line of your body, begin to exhale as you continue to the left, twisting your body with the movement of your hands. When you reach the full extent of your twist to the left, reverse your hands again.

Begin to inhale as you move your hands back to center.

Inner Space

If you imagine you are holding a 12-inch glowing golden ball, you will have no difficulty mastering this movement. Handle the ball with reverence as you feel the warmth of the energy you hold.

Projecting Light

STRETCHING BETWEEN HEAVEN AND EARTH

Technique

Slide your right foot out until your feet are shoulder width apart, and keep your hands at your sides. To begin, hold your hands in front of you with your palms down, fingers pointing toward each other, and elbows flexed. Inhale normally.

Exhale as you raise your left arm, with your palm pushing up toward the sky. At the same time, your right hand pushes down toward the earth. Twist as far as you can to your right, pushing your arms out to their extended position.

Inhale as you turn back to the front, your hands returning to the beginning position.

Exhale as you raise your right arm with your palm pushing up to the sky. At the same time, your left hand pushes down to the earth. Twist as far as you can to your left, pushing your arms out to their extended position.

Inhale as you turn back to the front as before.

Inner Space

Mother Earth is beneath you; Father Sky is above you. As you press upward and push downward with your hands, you are forming an energy bridge between the two opposites. The energy above you and below you blends within your own being.

Stretching Between Heaven and Earth

Snake Projects Chi

Pressing your thighs together and your arms against your body massages your lymph glands.

Technique

> Slide your right foot out; leave your hands at your sides. Turn your toes inward and press your thighs together firmly.
>
> Inhale and bring your hands up in front of you, palms facing each other, index and middle fingers upright, while pressing your arms snugly against your body. This hand position represents the snake.
>
> Exhale and push your arms straight out to the sides with your palms facing outward, maintaining the "snake" position of your hands.
>
> Rotate your wrists and open your hands, letting your palms face upward.
>
> Inhale, bringing your arms up and over your head.
>
> Exhale, bringing your hands down the center line of your body, close together but not touching, and back down to your sides.

Inner Space

As you bring your hands up on inhalation, you draw chi up your body. As you exhale, pressing out, you are powerfully projecting chi down your arms to your palms. Inhaling up, you bring chi up over your head and sweep energy down, infusing your aura with life force.

Snake Projects Chi

VERTICAL STRETCH

Technique

Slide your right foot out, and leave your hands at your sides.

Inhale, sweeping your hands straight up in front of you, with wrists dropped and fingers trailing. Continue to sweep your hands over your head where they then open out as wide as is comfortable, with your palms open to the sky.

Form "Cranes' Beaks" with your hands by holding your fingers to your thumbs. Bring these beaks down to touch your shoulders.

Exhale as you release the "Cranes' Beaks" and bring your hands to just below your chin. The backs of your hands will be facing but not touching. Your fingers will be pointing downward.

Push your hands down the center line of your body, fingertips first. Do not touch your body. As your arms reach their full extension, return your hands to your sides.

Inner Space

Feel the chi you are pulling in from the earth and the sky as it circulates down the line of your chakras to Manipura. Your central chakras are energized from your crown to your base.

Vertical Stretch

DRAWING THE BOW

This posture creates isometric tension throughout your body, releasing a rush of energy as you relax back to the center position. The only way to do this posture correctly is to really draw the bow. You should feel that you are exerting strength to pull the bowstring back. It may help to achieve the proper stance if you watch yourself in a mirror, or practice with a real bow.

Technique

Slide your right foot out until your feet are shoulder width apart. Your arms begin at your sides.

Inhale and twist to your right, drawing your left arm back so that your left hand "holds" the bowstring at the level of your jaw. Simultaneously push your right fist out to hold the "bow." Lean back slightly so that you are aiming at the sky.

Exhale as you turn to the front. Your hands will come back together, not touching, but in a relaxed, cupped position in front of Manipura.

Inhale and twist to your left, drawing your right arm back so that your left hand "holds" the bowstring and your right arm pushes out to hold the "bow."

Exhale as you turn back to center.

Inner Space

You are the Archer. Feel the bow in your hands, and the tension as you draw the bowstring back. The surge of life force energy builds as you pull the bow, and that chi rushes through your body as you relax.

Drawing the Bow

TIGER COMES OUT OF THE CAVE

Technique

Begin with your feet shoulder width apart and your hands at your sides.

Inhale and "scoop" energy up with your cupped hands, by reaching with them back, around, and up to the front.

Exhale as your hands strike out in front as "claws."

Inhale as you scoop your hands back and around again. As you bring your hands up, twist your torso to your right.

Exhale as you strike out to the right with clawed hands.

Inhale as you scoop your hands again. As your hands come up, twist around to your left.

Exhale as you strike out to your left.

Inhale as you scoop your hands and twist back to the center position.

Inner Space

You are a tiger. Your hands become claws as you strike out. Make a "tiger face" as you strike. Feel the power build with your inhalation and feel the chi surge through you as you exhale.

Tiger Comes Out of the Cave

CRANE DRAWS IN CHI

This movement is excellent for circulating excess energy if you start to feel shaky during any practice session.

Technique

Your feet remain together, and your hands at your sides. Face forward.

Inhale, bringing your hands up in front of your body, palms up.

Exhale, rotating your wrists so your palms are facing out, pushing your hands straight in front of you.

Inhale, relaxing your wrists and hands and letting your fingers trail as you sweep your arms straight up over your head. Then smoothly circle your hands out until they are at right angles to your body, with palms up.

Exhale, sweeping your hands back up above your head and then down slowly along the center line of your body (hands cupped slightly, not touching), and end with your hands at your sides again.

Inner Space

This movement circulates chi and helps it to flow evenly throughout the body and its meridians. The first inhalation pulls chi energy up your legs, and the first exhalation pushes that chi down your arms. The second inhalation brings the energy up to Sahasrara, your crown chakra. The final exhalation sweeps the chi force down to Manipura, your main power storage center. Try to follow this flow of chi with your visualization.

Crane Draws in Chi (Side and Front Views)

CIRCULATING THE LIGHT

Technique

Your feet remain together, and hands at your sides to begin.

Inhale, sweeping your arms up until they are above your head. Rise up on your toes as you do so.

Hold your hands about four inches apart and rotate them nine times, as though rolling a ball between your palms.

Exhale, sweeping your hands down in front of you (without touching each other or your body) and back to your beginning position. Lower your heels until they are once again on the ground.

Inhale, sweeping your arms up and standing on your toes.

Rotate your hands nine times as before, this time in the opposite direction.

Exhale and return to the beginning position.

Inner Space

As you rise on your toes and sweep your hands upward, feel that you are bringing chi or pranic energy up your body and into your hands to Lao Kun, the palm chakras. As you rotate your hands, visualize that you are rolling a small, golden, glowing ball of energy between your palms. As you bring your hands down, chi flow follows your hands down your body meridians to Manipura.

Circulating the Light

T'ai Chi Ruler

The Chinese word T'ai Chi means "universe" and is a philosophy conceived by the ancient Chinese to describe the cosmos. T'ai Chi Chuan, perhaps the most familiar form of T'ai Chi to Americans, means an exercise, or chuan, which attempts to relate the universe to the individual. Probably first taught as a system of self-defense, T'ai Chi Chuan later evolved into a system of meditative exercise to improve health. It increases strength, coordination, endurance, and grace, while improving the respiratory and cardiovascular systems of the body. These systems seem to slow the effects of our stress-filled, inactive Western way of life the most.

T'ai Chi Ruler is another form of Chinese meditative exercise, using a short stick of wood called a ruler. These movements are similar in some ways to T'ai Chi Chuan, but we believe T'ai Chi Ruler has several advantages. It requires less space to perform, good results can be achieved with shorter daily practice sessions, and it can be used even by bedridden or handicapped individuals (as long as they can move their arms). The same benefits accrue: increased flexibility, strength, coordination, and grace. The tranquility of the exercises seems to carry over into daily life.

It is unknown who invented the ruler used in these exercises. The ruler is made of wood and is approximately 10½ inches long. It acts as an energy conductor which creates a bridge as it is held between Lao Kun, the palm chakras of your hands. The shape of the ruler is said to have mystical significance as well. For this reason, even though you can substitute any short stick or dowel, you may wish to use the traditionally-shaped ruler. Please see the Appendix for information on obtaining one.

As you do the T'ai Chi Ruler movements, synchronized with the breath, you are drawing chi up through the chakras of your feet (Bubbling Spring), along the meridians of your legs, and up through Manipura. The flow continues up through Anahata and down your arm meridians to Lao Kun, your palm chakras, which are bridged by the ruler to allow energy flow in both directions.

During each sequence, your attention should remain on Manipura, where you imagine a glowing light. Your peripheral awareness will still be able to follow the energy flowing along your meridians. Stand relaxed, pelvis slightly tucked, back straight. Your breathing pattern throughout will be to inhale when the ruler comes close to your body, and to exhale when it moves away from you.

Occasionally, some students may find that their hands become cold after a few movements. If this happens, you will need to modify your visualization. Proceed as usual, but besides maintaining your awareness at Manipura, consciously follow the energy down your arm meridians to Lao Kun. Maintain in your imagination a warm, glowing, golden light collecting between your hands. At first, it may seem complex to visualize a light both at Manipura and at Lao Kun, but do not underestimate your capabilities with creative visualization. Having two focal points will become natural very quickly, and after a few movements you will find your hands will become warm.

T'ai Chi Ruler exercises are best performed to slow, tranquil music. Each individual's speed of movement will vary, but the flow of movement is generally slow, graceful, and smooth, paced by controlled breathing, promoting inner serenity. The serenity attained during the exercises should continue long after the practice session is complete.

STANDING FORM 1

Stand relaxed, holding the ruler between your palms in front of you. The ruler is parallel to the ground. Your feet are about shoulder width apart. Turn your right foot so it is at an angle to your left foot. Your body will face slightly to your right.

Start with the ruler at the level of Manipura, your solar plexus. Begin to move the ruler first out and away from your body, and continue to describe a complete circle until the ruler returns to Manipura again. The ruler is moved down when it is close to your body and then up when away from your body. As the ruler moves down and is close to your body, lean slightly back and inhale. As the ruler moves up, away from your body, lean slightly forward and exhale. Repeat 9, 18, or 36 times.

Reverse the direction of the circle you describe. The ruler now moves up when it is close to your body and down when away from it. Lean slightly back and inhale when the ruler is close to your body. Lean slightly forward and exhale when the ruler is away from you. Repeat the circle the same number of times as before.

Return to the beginning position. Slightly change the direction you are facing by turning your left foot at an angle to the right foot. Your body will face to your left.

Repeat the complete exercise from this new position.

Standing Form 1

STANDING FORM 2

Stand relaxed, holding the ruler between your palms in front of you. The ruler is parallel to the ground and your feet are about shoulder width apart, as in Form 1. This exercise, however, is performed from only one position, where the ruler describes a circle directly in front of you.

Starting with the ruler at the level of Manipura, move the ruler first out and away from your body in a downward direction, describing a small circle at first. As in Form 1, inhale as the ruler moves down and is close to your body. Exhale when the ruler is coming up and away from your body. The circle begins quite small and is performed slowly. Gradually make the circle larger and your circular motion will speed up proportionately. After the circle reaches its largest size, gradually reduce it and slow the speed of the ruler until you gracefully come to a stop. Do not attempt to count the number of revolutions, but rather concentrate on the waxing and waning of the circle.

Now perform exactly the same sequence, but this time move the ruler in the opposite direction. The ruler will move up when close to your body, and down when away from it. One complete set of the exercise has been performed when you come to a halt the second time.

Standing Form 2

STANDING FORM 3

Stand relaxed, the ruler (parallel to the ground) between your palms, and your feet shoulder width apart. Begin to draw a circle with the ruler, this time bringing it up from Manipura as you inhale. Bring the ruler up close to your body, near your head. Then exhale as you continue down with the large circle. As you lower the ruler away from your body, bend over toward your feet. Stop bending when the ruler is almost to your feet. Start inhaling as you continue around the big circle, with the ruler close to your legs as you raise your body gradually to an upright position. Continue describing this large forward circle for 9, 18, or 36 repetitions to complete one set of this exercise.

STANDING FORM 4

This form is the same as Form 3, except that as you inhale and raise the ruler up to start the circle, you must bring it up over your head until your arms are fully extended, and stand up on your toes at the same time. Make a stretch out of this motion. Then, as you lower the ruler in a circular motion away from your body and downward, exhale and come back down on your heels. Lower the wand as far as your arms will allow. Continue this version of the large circling motion for 9, 18, or 36 repetitions to complete one set of the exercise.

Standing Form 3

Standing Form 4

STANDING FORM 5

This is the same exercise as the Projecting Light exercise of T'ai Chi Chi Kung, except that you now have the ruler, instead of a ball of energy, between your hands.

Stand relaxed, holding the ruler between your palms. Inhale, and at the level of Manipura, rotate your hands so your left hand is uppermost, with its palm downward. Your right hand will be palm upward. Exhale as you twist smoothly to your right, rotating your arms to the right and keeping your hands in the same position. When you have twisted as far as you can, reverse your hands so that the right hand is on top.

Begin to inhale as you move your hands back toward the center. When you reach the center line of your body, begin to exhale as you continue on to the left, twisting your body with the movement of your hands. When you have twisted as far as you can, reverse your hands so the left hand is uppermost. Begin to inhale as you move your hands back to the center. Repeat the entire sequence 9, 18, or 36 times to make one complete set of the exercise.

Standing Form 5

SITTING FORM 1

Sit on a stool, a chair, or the side of a bed. You do not want your feet to touch the floor. Curve your feet and toes upward slightly, creating tension on your hamstring muscles.

Hold the ruler in front of you, parallel to the ground. Inhale and move it close to your body, beginning the first part of the circle. Continue around and begin to exhale as the ruler comes down. Do not touch the ruler to your body, but involve your upper body and arms as much as possible in making a large, smooth circle, leaning backward and forward slightly as necessary. Repeat the circle 9, 18, or 36 times. Reverse the direction of the circle and repeat it the same number of times to complete one set of this exercise.

SITTING FORM 2

Sit on the floor or on a firm bed with your legs stretched out in front of you. Describe a large circle in the usual way, moving upward and inhaling, continuing around the circle, and going down while exhaling. Do not touch your body or legs with your hands, but try to use as much of your body as possible, working, stretching, extending your arms and your upper body. Describe the large circle 9, 18, or 36 times. Reverse the direction of the circle and repeat it the same number of times to complete one set of this exercise.

Sitting Form 1

Sitting Form 2

PRONE POSITION FORM 1

Lie flat on your back on the ground, the floor, or a firm bed. With your elbows bent and resting up against your sides, hold the ruler at the level of Manipura. Describe a circle in the usual way, coming up close to your body at first and inhaling. Continue around with a small circle, exhaling as the ruler moves toward your feet. Repeat the circle 9, 18, or 36 times.

Reverse the direction of the circle and repeat the same number of times, for one complete set of this exercise.

PRONE POSITION FORM 2

This exercise is almost the same as Form 1, except that you reach above your head with the ruler and down toward your feet, extending your arms as far as possible each time. Begin by moving the ruler toward your head and inhaling, then exhaling as the ruler starts toward your feet. Repeat this large circle 9, 18, or 36 times.

Reverse the direction of the circle and repeat the same number of times, for one complete set of this exercise.

Prone Position Form 1 and Form 2

Earth Dancing with a Partner

Earth Dancing

Earth Dancing is commonly known as the belly dance of the Middle East. This dance form focuses on a great deal of movement in the hip and pelvic area. Dances from all over the world use similar movements, including African, Polynesian, and Spanish forms of dance.

Throughout history, many if not most cultures have used the "trance" dance. This is a dance with music and often with drum accompaniment, perhaps with the eyes closed. The attention must be focused inward. It is possible to achieve a deep state of meditation this way.

Besides achieving meditative goals, dance can also be an effective form of physical exercise. What makes Earth Dancing superior to other dance or exercise forms is the focus on the hips and pelvis. Many of us are very tight and stiff in this area. You will notice this inflexibility when you start to practice the movements. Gradually your tight muscles will relax into a new freedom of movement.

Earth Dancing also tones the internal organs, massaging them through movement, through the tension and relaxation of muscles in the pelvic area. Traditionally, this form of dance was used to prepare a woman for childbirth, toning and strengthening this area of her body. The energy required during an average childbirth is estimated to be equivalent to that needed when running a six mile race.

The music used for Earth Dancing, as in all meditative dance, is important. The selection must be made with care. We do not advise using modern popular music; with few exceptions, it is generally not sufficiently relaxing nor conducive to a meditative state of mind. New Age and ethnic music offer the most possibilities. Be creative. Besides the obvious choice of Middle Eastern music, you can also try Native American drum and flute music, African drum music, East Indian music, even Renaissance music. Middle Eastern music is probably the best to begin with. Music with a relaxed, slow, and sensuous rhythm should be chosen, which will encourage the right feelings for relaxing and moving your body.

Earth Dancing Instruments

Sufi Drumming

The drum has been an inseparable accompaniment to ancient trance dancing techniques. Many different drums have been developed in Africa; and there are the drums of Native Americans, and the Doumbeck of the Middle East, to name just a few. Each different drum has a different sound.

Here we will show you a method of trance drumming from the Sufi tradition. Ideally, you should use the hourglass-shaped Doumbeck. However, any drum with a leather (or synthetic) head at least ten inches in diameter will work.

If you have experience with drumming, even if you are one of the greatest drummers ever, please put that experience aside for the moment. Try to approach this technique as if you are picking up a drum for the first time. This method of drumming is meant to put the drummer, as well as anyone present, into a state of meditation. With embellishment and variation, it can also be used for many other kinds of dancing.

Hold the Doumbeck between your legs as you kneel, or stand or sit with it under one of your arms. Find the position that is most comfortable for you and produces a clear, resonating tone. Remove any rings to avoid damaging your drum.

To help you quickly learn the drumming pattern, each area of the drum has a name. These directions are for right-handed drummers, so please reverse the directions if you are left-handed.

Tapping the center of the drum produces a dull sound, and we refer to striking the drum in the center as "boom." Always strike "boom" with your right hand. The right side of the drum near the edge produces a lighter tone, and we will always refer to striking the drum on the right edge as "tuck." Always strike "tuck" with your right hand. Some teachers prefer "doom tek," so select the terms that seem most comfortable to you.

Striking the left side of the drum near the edge is indicated by "ee," and is always struck with your left hand.

Your right hand strikes only "booms" and "tucks." Your left hand strikes "ees." Always say the name of each area as you practice. It may sound silly to do so, but this makes it easier to keep track of the correct sound pattern, and it also keeps your drumming from getting too fast.

First, strike the center of the drum and say "boom." Continue striking the center and saying "boom" each time, getting comfortable with holding the drum. Try to develop a steady, unrushed beat. If you think your rhythm isn't quite steady enough, practice while watching the second hand of a clock. Synchronize each "boom" with each second that passes, until you learn to keep a steady tempo. Now, strike the center of the drum, "boom," and then with your same hand, strike the right edge, "tuck." Say "boom;" say "tuck." Continue in an even rhythm between "boom" and "tuck" for several minutes.

The first pattern to learn is "boom-boom tuck." This is also the first half of the drumming pattern you will use (Pattern 1) until you don't have to think about what your hands are doing. Always say the names out loud. Patterns 2 through 4 prepare you for the last half of the final drumming pattern. Work your way through each preparatory pattern so that you can put the final pattern together easily.

Pattern 2 consists of "boom tuck-tuck-tuck" repeated over and over. Say each name, and keep the rhythm steady. You will strike three "tucks" in the same amount of time that you give for one "boom," still just using your right hand.

In Pattern 3 you finally use your left hand for "ee." The words are "boom-tuck-ee boom-tuck-ee." Each strike of the drum lasts the same length of time in this pattern. Spend some time getting used to using both hands.

Pattern 4 is "boom tuck-ee tuck-ee tuck-ee." The last strike "ee" lasts twice as long as the other strikes. Continue until you have mastered Pattern 4, saying each word out loud, and keeping a steady rhythm.

Pattern 5 is the final drumming pattern: "boom-boom tuck, boom tuck-ee tuck-ee tuck-ee." If you have mastered each previous pattern, it will come easily. Remember to say each word out loud, and to keep a steady rhythm. If necessary, have someone who reads musical notation help you with the rhythms, and perhaps keep a beat going with another drum or by clapping along with you.

If you find the complete pattern simply too difficult, you may wish to drum without the left hand "ee" strike. In this case, you

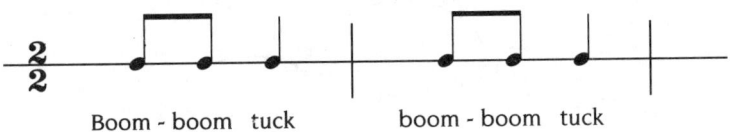

Boom - boom tuck   boom - boom tuck

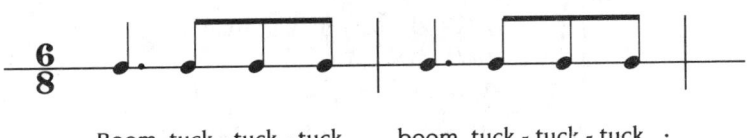

Boom tuck - tuck - tuck   boom tuck - tuck - tuck ·

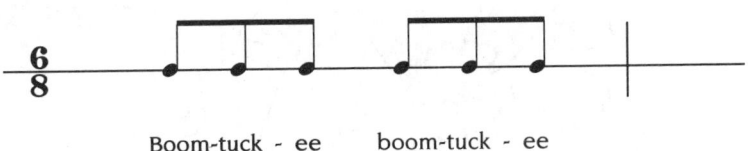

Boom-tuck - ee   boom-tuck - ee

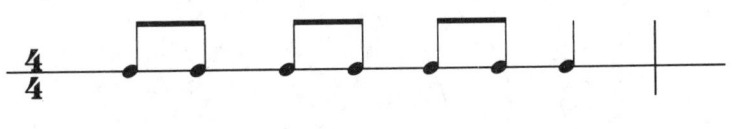

Boom tuck - ee   tuck - ee   tuck - ee

Boom - boom tuck, boom   tuck - ee   tuck - ee   tuck - ee

Earth Dancing Drum Patterns

Dancing with Zills

could drum Pattern 1 or 2 and still get a meditative effect. Do not give up completely, though. You may yet master the complete pattern if you continue to practice.

Now you will be ready to drum for as long as you like, taking yourself and those present into the realm of meditation.

Zills

Zills are tiny finger cymbals, about two inches in diameter, which make a wonderful accompaniment to Earth Dancing. They can be used by themselves, or with drums and a musical background.

To play the zills, you must first place them properly on your fingers. They are worn one on the thumb and one on the middle finger. Place the elastic around your finger so that it partially covers your fingernail. Make sure the elastic fits snugly. Place one set on each hand.

As a rule, you will want to clap the cymbals together on one hand, and then on the other, alternating back and forth. At first, try to alternate the ringing on each hand, working for a clear, bell-like tone. Tap the zills lightly together, experimenting until you obtain the clearest tone possible. Begin using them while you dance, keeping an even beat until you gain enough experience to begin experimenting with different sounds. There are no steadfast rules, and the advanced zills player can produce an infinite variety of sounds through variations of rings, taps, slides, etc., and ringing the zills alternately or simultaneously. For ideas, there are a number of master teachers who have produced teaching tapes and books.

Performing the Dance

To establish the proper atmosphere and put you in the right frame of mind for Earth Dancing, you might want to dress in loose pants or a flowing skirt, with finger cymbals and bangle jewelry. You do not want to feel restricted in any way. Also remember, whether you are male or female, large or small, your body is beautiful. Try to focus

Dancing from the Waist Up

on yourself, and let Earth Dancing reveal your beauty through its traditional movements.

To begin dancing, start your musical selection, then lie down and try to just "be" with the music. Breathe deep, relaxed breaths. Visualize the music entering and filling your body with light. When you are ready, do some stretching exercises, such as Yoga, which will loosen your muscles. Do these unhurriedly, perhaps for 15 or 20 minutes, or longer if you wish. This unwinding is essential.

Now sit in a relaxed, cross-legged position. Begin to allow your body to dance from the waist up. Allow sensuous arm movements; allow your head to move, your shoulders, your chest. Enjoy the relaxed movement. When you are ready, slowly stand.

BASIC PELVIC MOVEMENTS

Circles

Your knees should be slightly flexed and your feet about shoulder width apart. Move your hips around in a circle, as if you are drawing a circle that floats above the floor. Try to keep your upper body as motionless as possible. When you feel you have drawn your circle long enough in one direction, reverse and circle in the other direction. Stop and relax for a few moments.

You may want to tie a scarf firmly around your hips to help you focus your attention on your pelvis. Sometimes when you are first learning, it is also helpful to place your hands on your hips. Resting them just above your hips will help you keep your upper body still, and also helps you isolate movement in the pelvic area. You can also move your hands down lower on your hips, if you wish. For another change, try clasping your hands together over your head as you dance.

Figure Eights

For a figure eight movement of your hips, imagine that you are drawing lines with your hip joints. One side of your hip draws one loop of the eight, then the other hip draws the other loop. Continue drawing the figure eight unhurriedly as long as you wish. A variation

Hip Movements

is to lift your right heel, keeping your toes on the floor, and circle your right hip forward in one loop of the eight. Bring your heel back down as you finish the loop on that side. Your left foot has remained flat on the floor. Now reverse and lift your left heel while you draw the other loop with your left hip. As you finish one half of the movement, flow into beginning the other half of the movement. You can draw figure eights in both directions.

Hip Bump

Put weight on one foot, and bump your hip out to that side. The toes and ball of your other foot will brace against the floor and help push your hip out. A good way to practice this movement, if you are having difficulty, is to stand sideways next to a wall. Your hip should be about six inches to a foot away from the wall. Now "bump" sideways so your hip touches the wall. Start close and move away gradually as you get the feel of the side-to-side bumping and shifting of balance that is required. If you have someone to practice with, you can stand next to each other and bump hips. Make a real game of it; try to avoid the other person's "bumps" while you are trying to bump them. This is guaranteed to reduce even the most serious adults to giggling!

Once you have practiced regular bumping, try doing several bumps at a time on one side before shifting to the other side.

Another variation is called the pivoting hip bump. Keep one foot flat on the floor, to serve as a pivot. The other will circle around the pivot foot. As you pivot, your hip bumps out in a straight line from the center pivot foot. Your center pivot foot should remain flat on the floor as you bump your way around.

Pelvic Rock

Stand with your feet comfortably apart, and your toes gripping the earth or floor. Smoothly tilt the pelvis forward, then relax and repeat. Forward, thrust, relax; forward, thrust, relax. Change directions by shifting your feet, and do the "rock" again. Create your own variations by swaying, changing your hand movements, etc.

Many variations of these basic pelvic movements are possible. For example, imagine that you have crayons attached to your hip

Arm Movements

joints or to your tailbone, and draw shapes with them. Try not to be inhibited as you play with your body and find out what it will do.

ADDITIONAL TECHNIQUES

Belly Roll

This traditional movement is not difficult. As you breathe in deeply, push your belly out and your chest will drop down a bit. As you exhale, pull your belly inward while your chest comes up and out. Practice this for a few moments, then begin to push your belly out in a sensuous undulation. After some practice you will begin to achieve the traditional rolling effect.

Gliding Walk

Take a comfortable stance, shoulders back, with your arms relaxed at your sides. Now walk smoothly to the music, your toes touching down first as a ballerina would walk. Take longer and longer steps until you are gliding along gracefully, effortlessly. Your movement is so fluid that you could balance a crystal goblet on your head as you move. Bend your knees a bit; now point your toes a little and continue to glide in long, graceful, sensuous steps.

There are many variations to this walk. One is to walk placing one foot in front of the other, going up and back. Also, you may cross one foot over in front of the other, so that your hips sway from side to side as you move forward and back. Then try stepping sideways. One foot steps to the side and then the other follows it, almost meeting it before the first foot steps out to the side again. All the previous foot movements have sideways or diagonal variations. Now, let the technique go and just dance with the music!

Dance is joy
expressed through movement

Veil Dancing

Veil Dancing

All the movements outlined so far can be used in Veil Dancing. Ideally, you should have a veil made of silk chiffon or Chinese silk; however, you may use any piece of lightweight, silky fabric. Polyester chiffon works well. The fabric must float easily and seem to remain suspended in the air when tossed up.

Hold the veil lightly between your index and middle fingers. Your arms should be extended completely when you hold the ends of the fabric. This will mean a piece about three yards long, and about 2½ feet to a yard wide.

Now, use the gliding walk from regular Earth Dancing. Glide across the floor with the veil floating behind you. Let it float until you have a feeling for how it is handled; relax and enjoy the rippling flow of the fabric. Now, as you are moving, raise your arms and bring the floating veil over you until it is in front of you. Walk backward, letting the veil float. Raise your arms and bring the floating veil back over your head until it is behind you again.

Play with these movements for a while. Stay relaxed and do not take it seriously if, during the middle of your lyrical dance, your veil should get caught in your hair! When you feel more comfortable with the veil, try some of the pelvic movements as you hold it.

Many of the movements used for Red Dragon Chi Kung can also be used for Veil Dancing. Infinity is especially enjoyable with a veil. Just remember that the veil must always be handled calmly and peacefully, and its qualities of graceful fluidity will become a part of yourself.

Measuring the Veil

Chakra Energizers

The origin of these exercises is unclear. They were probably developed in Tibet or India, and are said to be part of an ancient and secret system of Yoga for physical rejuvenation. When practiced regularly, they do seem to have a powerful influence. Try them for at least a month and see how they work for you.

When you are in optimum health, your chakras spin at a high frequency of vibration. This frequency tends to lower with age and inactivity. When the spin of the chakras slows down, the result is an increasingly unresponsive endocrine system. The flow of hormones to regulate body functions is affected, and often the signals are ignored or misunderstood by other parts of the body. A domino effect begins to occur because the endocrine glands have a close partnership. If one is not working properly, it will influence the others.

The purpose of these exercises is to energize and restore the spin of the chakras to their youthful rate. This is a desirable outcome, because if the chakra system is perfectly balanced, it is said that the body will not age.

Each of the energizers is meant to be repeated 21 times to make a complete set. You should perform all five sets in the morning, and then again in the evening, if you wish.

Once you become proficient, you should be able to complete all five energizers in about 10 minutes. But in the beginning, you may have difficulty performing all the energizers perfectly and with this many repetitions.

Do not become impatient with your progress. Do the best you can, and gradually the exercises will become easier. Start by performing each energizer just three times. Increase by adding two or more repetitions with each week of practice. They should be done at a speed comfortable for you, but do be careful to fully inhale and fully exhale as you do them.

Energizer 1 uses no energy locks. All the rest require that you maintain Moola bandha (root lock) throughout. Let your breathing pattern establish the rhythm for performing 2 through 5.

ENERGIZER 1

Using no locks, stand erect with your arms outstretched at shoulder level. Your right hand is turned palm up, your left hand is turned palm down. Now spin in a clockwise direction (to your right). Choose something in the room at eye level and count each time you pass it. Spin at a comfortable speed until you feel a little dizzy, up to 21 times.

Please remember that this is not the same movement as the Sufi Whirling meditation. The differences are subtle but critical in achieving the goal of each exercise.

ENERGIZER 2

Lie flat on the floor on your back. Your arms should be along your sides, with your palms on the floor. Maintain Moola bandha. Inhale and raise your head off the floor, bringing your chin firmly against your chest. As you raise your head, also lift your legs as high off the floor as possible. Don't let your knees bend. Now, exhale and lower both your head and legs back to the floor. Repeat up to 21 times. Remember to breathe in when your head and legs are raised, and breathe out as you lower them.

ENERGIZER 3

Kneel with your body upright, with your hands behind you against the backs of your thighs. Maintain Moola bandha. Inhale normally. Exhale and lower your head so your chin is pressed firmly against your chest. Then inhale as you vigorously bend your head and neck backward, arching your spine. This should create a stretch from your stomach to your chin. Your hands will act as a brace against your thighs to support the arching movement. Repeat up to 21 times.

Chakra Energizer 1

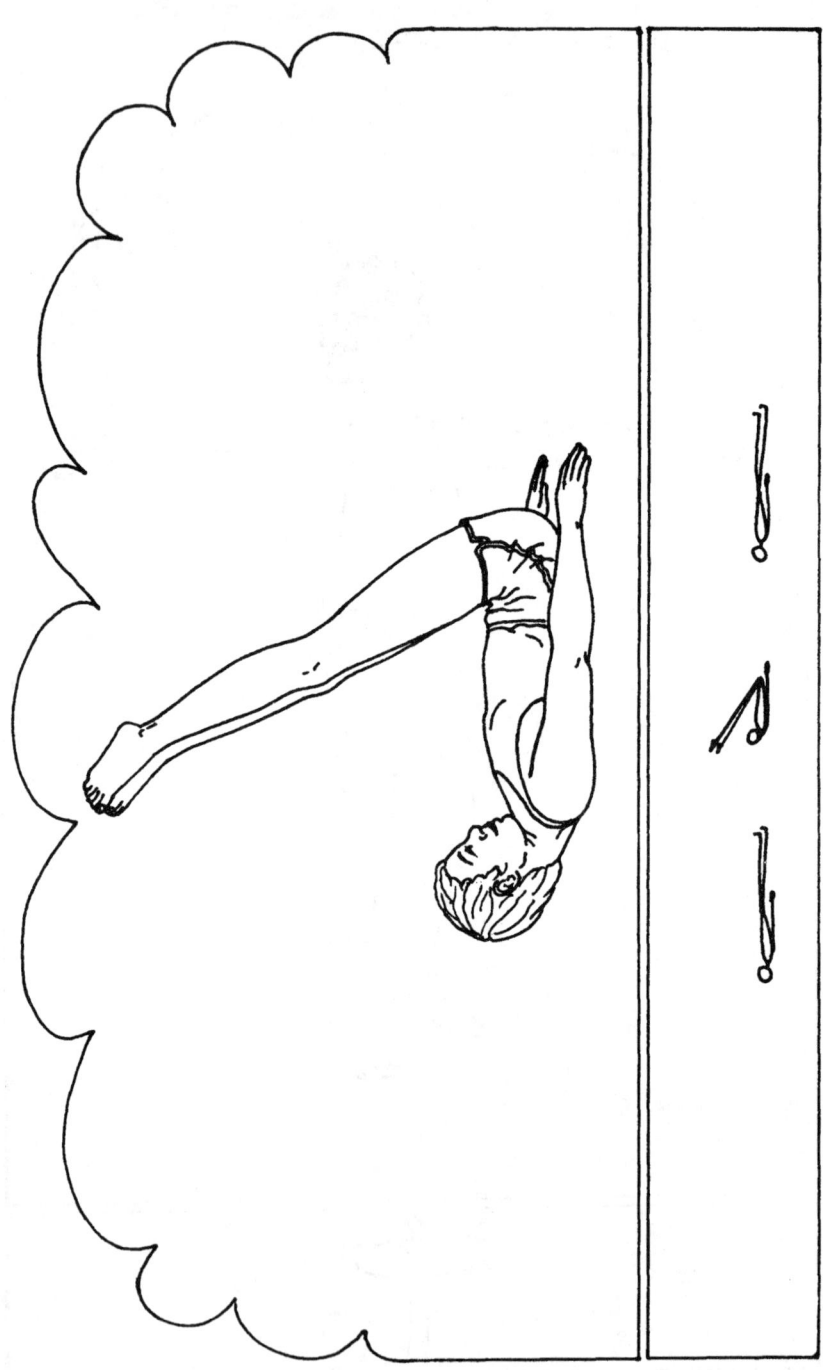

Chakra Energizer 2

Chakra Energizer 3

ENERGIZER 4 .

Sit on the floor with your legs straight in front of you and your feet about 12 inches apart. Your upper body is held erect. The palms of your hands are resting on the floor beside your hips. Maintain Moola bandha. Inhale normally, then exhale and tuck your chin down firmly to your chest. Inhale and toss your head backward as far as it will comfortably go, at the same time raising your body off the floor. Your knees will be bent and your arms will be straight. The trunk of your body will be parallel to the floor while your arms and lower legs will be perpendicular to the floor. Tense your muscles while in this position, then relax and exhale as you return to the sitting position you started with. Repeat this exercise up to 21 times.

ENERGIZER 5

Lie face down on the floor. Bend your elbows and place your hands flat on the floor by your shoulders. Your feet will be about one foot apart. Maintain Moola bandha. Inhale normally. Exhale, lift your head, and push up with your arms so that you are balanced on your hands and toes. Tense your muscles for a second. Now, push your hips up away from the floor, inhaling as you do so. You will be creating an inverted "v" shape with your body, your chin pulled firmly against your chest. Tense your muscles again. Repeat up to 21 times. Ideally, no other part of your body should touch the floor except your hands and toes as you flex your body back and forth between the head up position and the inverted "v."

Chakra Energizer 4

Chakra Energizer 5

ENERGY CIRCULATOR

After you have completed the Chakra Energizers, take a moment to circulate the energy you have generated. Perform the following exercise (which is presented also in the T'ai Chi Chi Kung section) three times. No locks are used.

Crane Draws in Chi

Standing with slightly bent knees, inhale through your nose as you lift your hands to waist level. Your elbows should be bent, and your palms up. Exhale, pushing out to the front with your hands, palms facing forward. Inhale and raise your arms up to the cosmos, palms up. Exhale as you bring your hands down. Repeat two more times to complete the circulation of chi.

Indian Isometrics

In our Western lifestyle, many of us spend the greater part of our waking lives sitting, often hunched over something in front of us. This causes our neck and shoulders to become tense and stiff, and there is no free physical movement or energetic flow. When your muscles are stiff, the energy channels become blocked, in turn affecting the organs, glands, and nerves into which these channels feed.

The following are isometric exercises from the traditions of East India. They use dynamic tension to energize and relax the body. When you work the muscles against each other isometrically, the tension briefly restricts blood and chi flow. When the tension is relaxed, the muscles receive a rush of oxygen-rich blood and chi. This alternation of tension and relaxation, of deprivation and replenishment of your body's physical and spiritual life forces, leaves you energized; your muscles will also be much looser than before.

These exercises take so little time and space that they could even be performed on your coffee or lunch break at work. Have your beverage when you pause from working if you wish, but add some isometrics for even more refreshment for your body. These exercises are also an excellent preliminary for any other set of exercises.

STRETCHING UP 1

Stand relaxed, with your arms at your sides. Inhale and sweep your arms up from your sides until they are overhead, at the same time going up on your toes. When your hands reach above your head, press your palms together to create isometric tension in your arms. Hold your breath while in this position for a moment. Take a small sniff of air to allow an even exhalation, then exhale as you lower your arms and come down from your toes. When your hands have just separated but are still facing overhead, rotate your wrists so your palms point away from each other. Continue to lower your arms until they are down to your sides.

Perform the stretch seven times, then relax. This exercise will help open the front of your lungs.

STRETCHING UP 2

Perform the stretch as in Stretching Up 1, except for a different hand position. This time, press the backs of your hands together. Inhale as you go up, press the backs of your hands together, maintain the tension for a few moments, then exhale and come back down. Perform the stretch seven times, then relax.

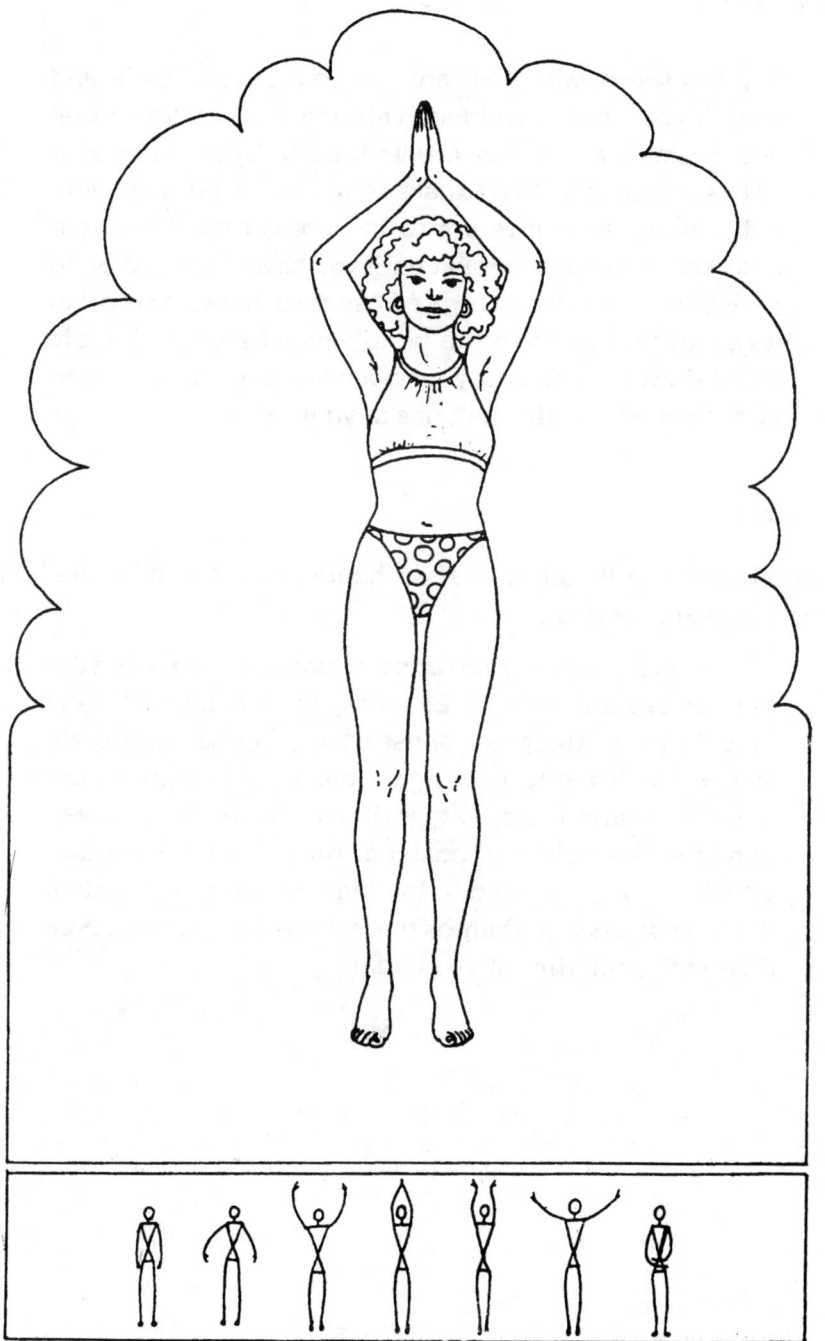

Stretching Up 1

SIDEBENDS 1

Stand relaxed, with your arms at your sides. Inhale and
stretch your arms overhead, crossing your wrists so that
your palms are together. Create tension by pressing your
palms together tightly. Exhale as you bend slowly to your
right. Inhale as you return to the upright position, your
arms still overhead. Repeat until you have done the bend
seven times to the right. Recross your hands the other
way, and now perform the bend seven times to the left.
Maintain the tension at your palms throughout the exercise, then relax with your arms at your sides.

VARIATION

Use this exercise if your wrists and hands are too stiff for the hand
position in Sidebends 1.

Inhale and stretch your arms overhead, hooking your
thumbs around each other, with your remaining fingers
free. Pull your thumbs against each other as you exhale
and bend slowly to your right. Inhale and return to the
upright position. Repeat until you have done seven
bends to the right. Rehook your thumbs from the other
direction and now bend to the left seven times. Maintain
the tension on your thumbs throughout the exercise, then
relax with your arms at your sides.

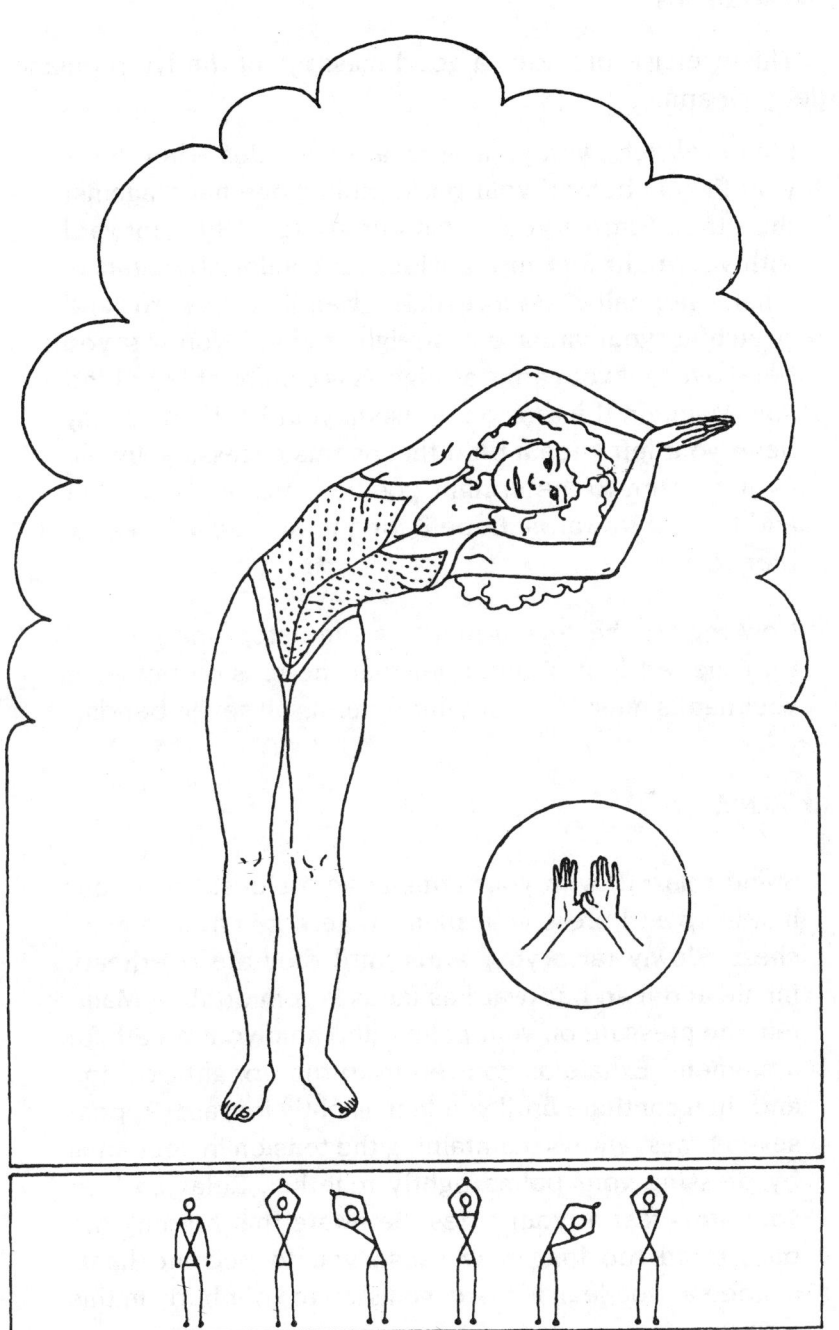

Sidebends and Variation

FORWARD BENDS

This exercise provides a good massage of the lymph glands under your arms.

Stand relaxed, with your arms at your sides. Then hook your fingers behind your back, pulling one hand against the other. Stretch your arms out straight. Step forward with your right foot into a wide but comfortable stance. Inhale normally, then exhale, bending forward and stretching your arms out straight behind you. As you bend over, lift your arms as high as is comfortable behind you. Maintain the tension between your hands. You may bend your left knee a bit if that seems necessary. Inhale as you return to the upright position, arching back a bit and looking upwards. Repeat for a total of seven bends, then relax.

Now repeat the technique, this time stepping forward with the left foot. Remember that the tension between your hands must be maintained during all seven bends.

BACK BENDS

Stand relaxed, with your arms at your sides. Bring your hands up and press your palms together in front of your chest. Slowly raise your arms until they are overhead. Inhale and lean backward as far as is comfortable. Maintain the pressure on your palms, and hold your breath for a moment. Exhale as you return to the upright position and then continue until you lean slightly forward. Repeat seven times, always maintaining the tension in your arms by pressing your palms tightly together. Relax and let your arms rest at your sides. Be aware that holding the back bend too long may cause you to become light-headed as you lean forward, so listen to your body in this respect.

Forward Bends

Back Bends

SPINAL TWIST

You should try to do the entire sequence on one inhalation, but if you run out of air, catch a quick sniff. This exercise should not be rushed.

Lie face down on the ground, with your arms at your sides and close to your body. Inhale and slowly raise your torso as you arch your back and look up. At the same time, bring your hands up and place them flat on the ground, just under your shoulders. Continue to inhale as you slowly extend your arms and push your body for more of an arch in your back, as you look up at the ceiling.

Still retaining your breath, slowly twist to one side and look behind you. Return to the front. Twist to the other side and look behind you. Return to the center.

Exhale, slowly returning to the face down position and returning your arms to your sides. Perform this exercise a total of seven times, then relax.

Spinal Twist

Yoga

Yoga literally means "union." The practices were developed in India to enable the practitioner to achieve union with the ultimate reality. Traditionally included are breathing exercises, mantras, meditation, and specific behavioral restraints. Here, we will only deal with a few of the physical exercises, which are unsurpassed as warm-up exercises.

Yoga exercises generally help make the body strong and flexible. They balance the physical areas of the body by regulating glandular secretions, toning muscles and nerves, massaging internal organs, and improving digestion and circulation. All the following Yoga poses can be performed by women during menstruation, except the Bow. The Cat and the Butterfly are very helpful during this time for most women.

Yoga exercises should be practiced at a slow pace, deliberately, with each pose being held for 20 seconds or more. If your breath is held during the pose, then the length of time you can comfortably hold your breath determines the length of time you can hold the pose.

As you hold each pose, try to relax as much as possible into the pose. If regularly practiced, this method of exercise is very calming. For a nervous or hyperactive individual, performing Yoga first can loosen muscles and calm the mind before going to a more active form of exercise.

BACK STRETCH

This pose gives a wonderful stretch to the spine and the legs, and firms the abdomen.

> Sit on the ground with your legs and feet together, and your spine straight. As you inhale, slowly raise your arms above your head, bend slightly backward, and stretch to the sky. Slowly bend forward, keeping your arms outstretched. Stop when you feel a stretch of the muscles in your back and legs. Reach down with your hands and grasp whatever part of your legs is comfortably within reach at the limit of your stretch. This may be your calves, ankles, or your feet. If you are very flexible, you may even be able to place your hands on the ground under your feet.

> When you have grasped whatever portion of your legs your flexibility allows, exhale. Relax your spine and head, and let them drop as close to your legs as they will go. Hold this pose and breathe long, relaxed breaths. Slowly rise to your original sitting position. Repeat this pose three times.

HEAD TO KNEE

This pose give a stretch to the spine and legs, and firms the abdomen.

> Lie on your back. Inhale and draw your left knee up to your chest, pulling it as close as is comfortable with your clasped hands. Raise your head as close to the knee as you can. Your right leg will remain straight on the ground. Hold your breath in the pose. Then, exhale while lowering your leg and your head back to the ground. Repeat this pose with the right leg, and then with both legs together. Go through the sequence one to three times.

Back Stretch

Head to Knee

COBRA

This pose stretches the spine and expands the chest.

Lie face down on the ground, placing the palms of your hands on the ground beside your shoulders. Inhale, slowly raising your head and chest off the floor. Arch backward as far as is comfortable. Continue to hold the pose, stretching and looking up and back. Then exhale and slowly return to the face down position. Perform up to three times.

PLOW

This pose makes your spine flexible, tones your back muscles, and helps to regulate the thyroid and parathyroid glands.

Lie on your back, with your arms alongside your body, palms down. Brace your palms against the ground, inhale, and start to bring your legs up. Pushing against the ground with your hands, continue to swing your legs up as slowly as possible. Bring them over until, if possible, you touch the ground behind your head with your toes.

Keep your legs straight at all times.

Hold the stretch, then exhale as you slowly come back to the original position. If you cannot lower your legs so that your toes rest on the floor behind your head while you hold the pose, find something of the right height to rest your toes on. Sometimes it is good to have a friend to help you master the bend of this exercise at first.

Cobra

Plow

BOW

This pose will help keep your entire body flexible, as well as strengthen your spine.

> Lie face down on the ground, with arms at your sides. Bend your knees and reach back to grasp your ankles. Inhale and lift your head, chest, and thighs off the floor as high as is comfortably possible. Tip your head back and hold your breath while you maintain the pose. Exhale slowly, releasing your hands gracefully and coming back down to the ground with your body. Repeat the pose two more times if you wish.

CAT

This pose strengthens your back and abdomen muscles, as well as flexing and toning your spine and its related muscles. It is very good for women during menstruation or pregnancy.

> Kneel on all fours with your hands and knees three to four inches apart on the ground. Your arms and thighs will be perpendicular to the ground; your back parallel to the ground. Inhale through pursed lips with a hissing sound. At the same time, arch your back up like an angry cat, lowering your head down to your chest until you can tuck your chin into the notch of your collarbone. Hold the pose. Exhale through your mouth as you raise your head and flex your back in the other direction by looking up until you get a good pull from your chin to your pubic bone. This back and forth flexing should be done slowly, with the rhythm of your breath, for several complete repetitions.

Bow

Cat

HALF SPINAL TWIST

This twist gives strength and flexibility to your spine while also drawing a fresh supply of blood to the area.

Sit on the ground with your right leg bent in front of you so your right heel is alongside your left hip. Lift your left foot over the folded right leg and place it flat on the ground beside your right thigh. Take a firm hold of your right knee with your right hand. Slowly inhale as you twist your torso to the left and reach behind you with your left hand, grasping your right side at the waist. Twist as far as is comfortable, keeping your spine straight. Exhale and slowly untwist and relax. Repeat the twist in the opposite direction, so that your left leg lies bent on the ground, with your right leg crossed over it. Repeat the entire exercise from one to three times.

BUTTERFLY

This pose stretches and tones your legs. For women, it is excellent for helping to regulate the menstrual cycle.

Sit on the ground, placing the soles of your feet together. As you become more flexible, your knees will begin to come close to touching the ground. Pull your heels in as close as possible to your body and grasp your feet with your hands. Inhale slowly and press your knees down toward the floor. Keep your entire spine and head in a straight line. Hold the position and breathe evenly and slowly, concentrating on Ajna, the third eye chakra. Release the position on the exhalation.

One variation is to place your hands on your knees and press down gently, instead of holding your feet. If this pose is comfortable for you, it can be maintained during passive meditation.

Half Spinal Twist

Butterfly

Cow's Head

This pose is good for relieving tension in the back and shoulders, and also strengthens the spine.

> Sit on the ground with your right leg bent in front of you so your right heel is alongside your left hip. Lift your left foot over the folded right leg and place it back alongside your right hip. Your left leg will be resting on top of your right leg. Raise your left arm overhead and then bend your elbow and reach behind your back. Come from below with your right hand and grasp your left hand, catching the fingertips together. Inhale and pull in opposite directions with your hands to create tension. Hold the position. Exhale slowly as you release your hands and relax.

> Reverse your legs and arms and repeat the pose. Go through the entire sequence from one to three times.

If your hands cannot grasp each other behind your back, use a piece of fabric to bridge the gap. Grasping each end of the fabric, pull from both directions so that your arm muscles are tensed. You may also sit in a comfortable cross-legged position until you become flexible enough to achieve this leg position.

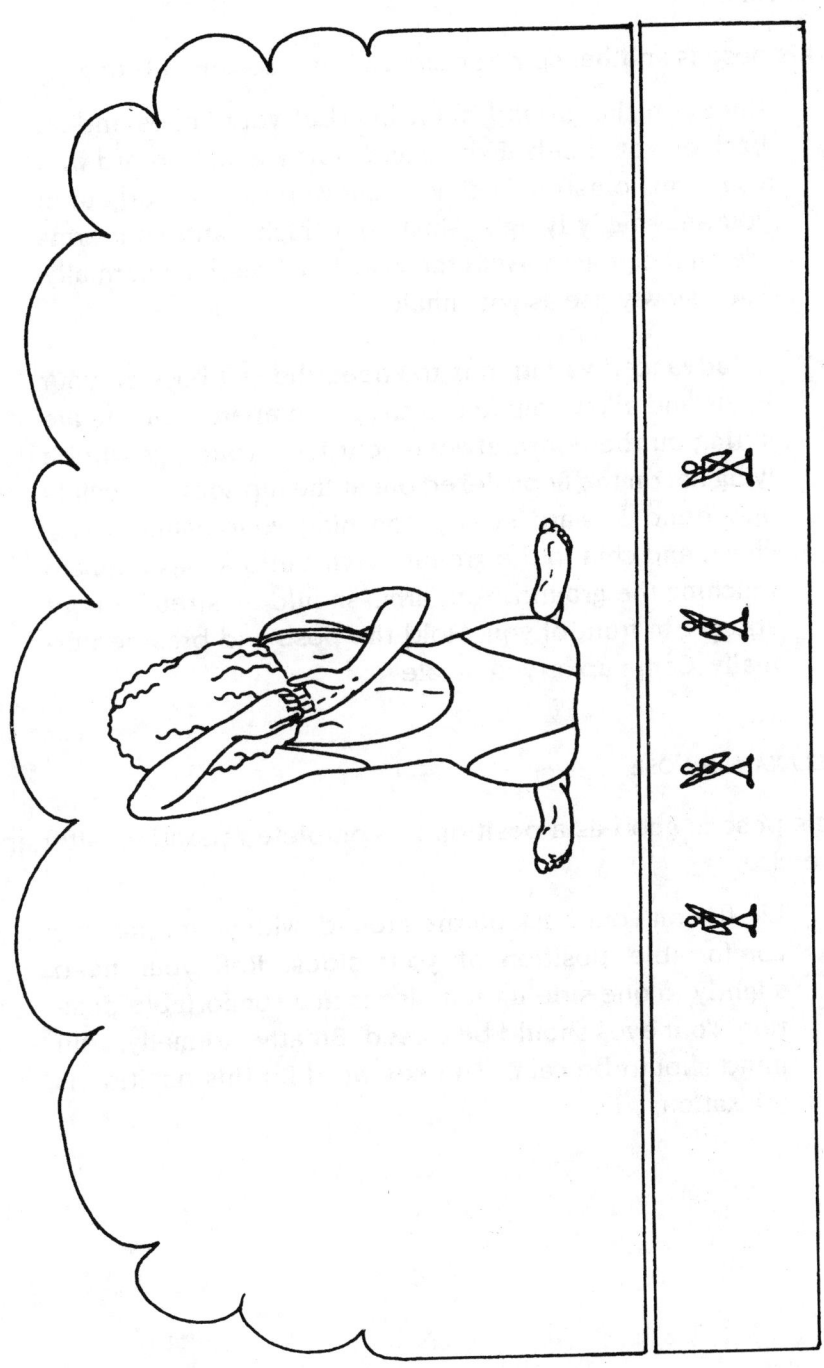

Cow's Head

TORTOISE

This pose is another spine stretcher. It is also very relaxing.

Kneel on the ground, then bend at your knees and sit back on your heels. Exhale and slowly bend forward with your arms outstretched. Relax, lowering your body until you are snugly lying against your thighs, and your arms are on the ground. Hold the position, breathing normally. Then slowly rise as you inhale.

An advanced variation is to kneel, then sit back on your heels and allow your knees to spread apart until you are sitting on the floor between your feet. Your legs will be lying flat on the floor, flexed out at the hip sockets. Exhale and bend forward slowly, touching your palms, arms, chest, and chin to the ground. Your buttocks also remain touching the ground. Your arms should be stretched out straight in front of you. Hold the pose and breathe normally. Come up as you inhale.

RELAXATION POSE

This pose is good as a position for complete relaxation, after any exercise.

Lie flat on your back on the ground, with your arms in a comfortable position at your sides. Roll your head slightly to one side until it also is in a comfortable position. Your eyes should be closed. Breathe normally. Your mind should be calm. The key word for this position is relaxation.

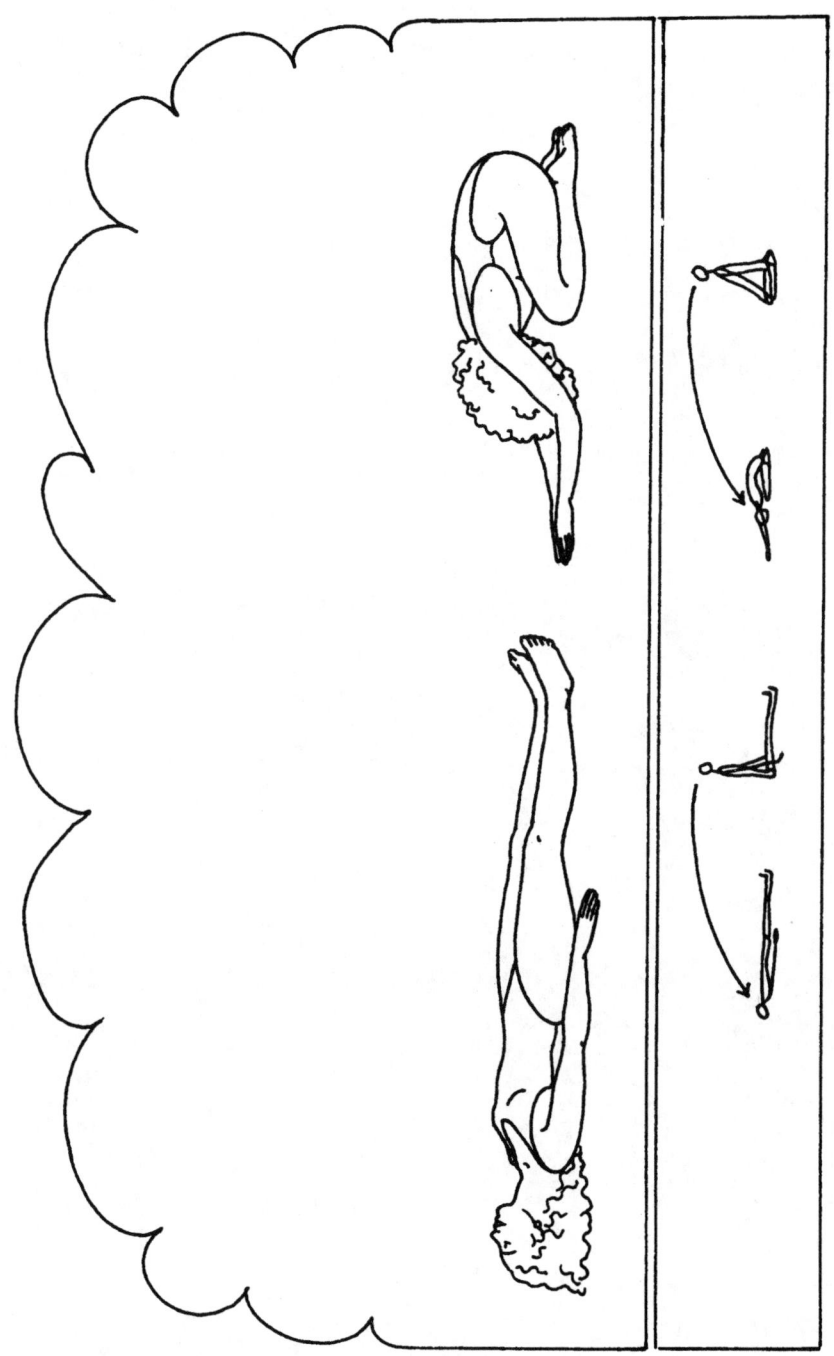

Relaxation and Tortoise Pose

Part Three

THE ALCHEMY

You may have already felt a change in your life from the steps taken down this spiritual path, the journey inward. A transformation or alchemy of spirit begins subtly and progresses gradually, so you may be uncertain as to the presence of any real change. Your detection circuits are used to measuring physical change, not spiritual change. Entering into meditation, which should be the beginning student's main goal, is the process of stepping beyond the physical into an unfamiliar world.

Meditation is being a witness to nothing; consciously doing something is not meditating. Use one of the devices we have suggested, or create one of your own. Then, hopefully, the alchemy of spirit will begin, and you will reach the threshold to meditation. Once so close, it becomes you who has to step across that threshold, from your accustomed state where it is you performing the action, to a state where you *are* the action.

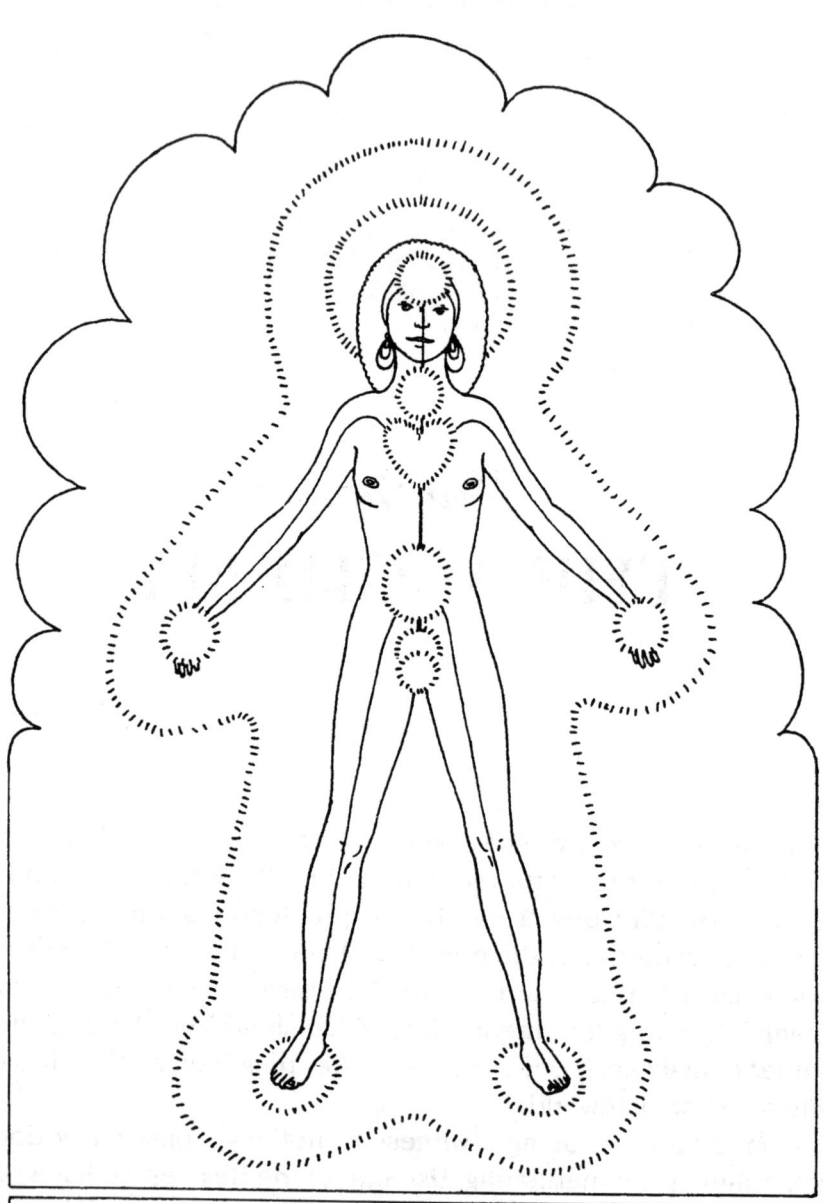

The Alchemy of Soul:
Bright chrysalis of spirit
Metamorphosis our goal.

Putting It All Together

We have attempted to share concepts, not hard and fast rules or details. There is no "right way" or "right system." There is not even a "right" way of structuring your individual exercise sessions.

Parts One and Two presented some of the elements and systems which people have used for the last several thousand years to attain spiritual growth. Tradition does lend these concepts some credibility, and they deserve respect. For that reason, before you change any part of these systems, examine them closely. Then make changes as necessary to achieve the results you desire.

A Sample Daily Program

Here is a possibility for one day's session of movement and breath. These elements and systems seem to fall together naturally. You may follow this pattern if you wish, or change the structure or sequence as needed.

Begin with Nadi Soghana, the breath of union. Then go to several Complete Breaths followed by a Cleansing Breath. You will want to be sitting on the ground or the floor.

Begin to move into some Yoga, slowly stretching and awakening your body. You might choose the Bow, the Cat, and the Half Spinal Twist, performing several repetitions of each. Return to a cross-legged position and perform the Dragon Breath, which prepares you for Red Dragon Chi Kung.

Rise and get your wand and go through all the Red Dragon Chi Kung exercises, with rhythmic musical accompaniment if possible. When these exercises are completed, remain on the ground. After pausing for a few moments, perform the Womb Meditation for as long as you wish. Then lie flat on your back in the Relaxation Pose from the Yoga section.

The entire sequence could be completed within one hour, but several hours set aside for spiritual work would not be too much.

Some Additional Beginnings

Here are some traditional stretching techniques which can be used in place of or in addition to Yoga when preparing for dynamic meditations such as Red Dragon Chi Kung, T'ai Chi Chi Kung, or T'ai Chi Ruler.

OPENING THE FOUR GATES

Sit or stand and turn your head as far as possible to the right. Then slowly turn your head as far to the left as possible. Now tilt your head back gently, as far as you can comfortably go. Slowly bend forward and tuck your chin firmly against your chest. Repeat this exercise slowly several times.

From a standing position, bend down until you can rest your hands on top of your knees. Now "draw" circles with your knees together, flexing and shifting with your hips. Circle first in one direction, then in the other. Repeat 9, 18, or 36 times.

From a standing position, rotate your shoulders by lifting and dropping them, first "drawing" forward circles 9, 18, or 36 times. Then repeat in the opposite direction, 9, 18, or 36 times.

From a standing position, twist your torso from one side to the other, loosening your waist area.

From a standing position, do some pelvic circles to loosen your hip area.

Opening the Four Gates

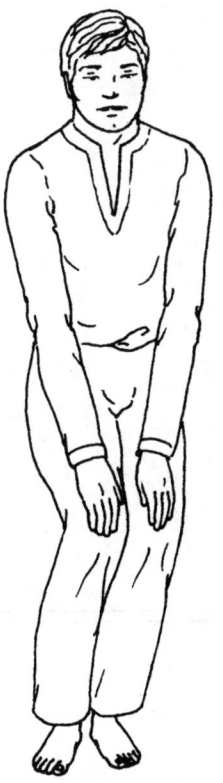

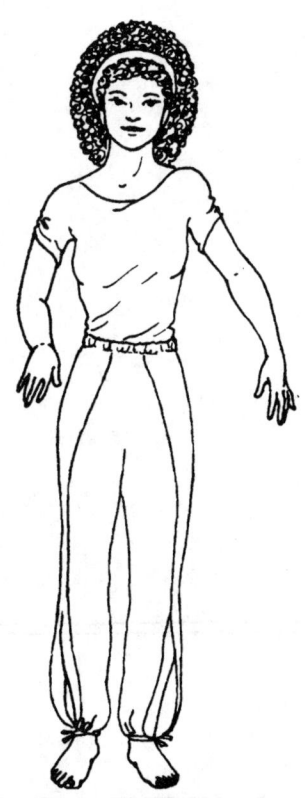

Drawing Circles with Knees   Rotating Shoulders

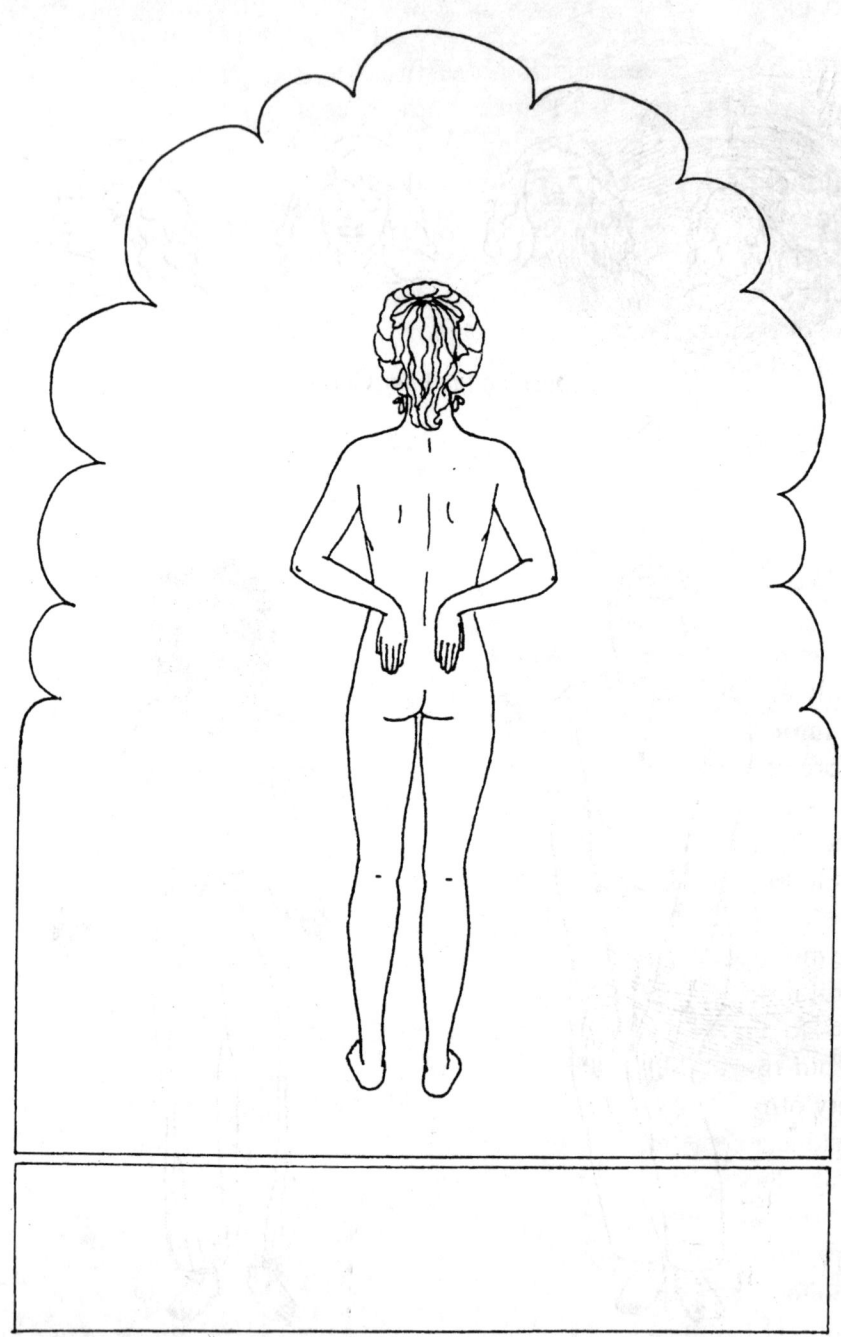

Sending Healing Energy to the Kidneys

CLOSING WITH HEALING ENERGY

To finish any exercise session of vigorous movement, it is beneficial to rub your kidney area. Think friendly thoughts about your kidneys as you rub in a circular motion over the kidney area. Send healing blue light energy into these vital organs, which are important to your total body health.

If you feel tenseness and/or soreness anywhere after doing your exercises, you can send this healing energy through your Lao Kun, or palm chakras, to whatever part of your body you touch. Use the healing blue light visualization to encourage this flow. After each session of movement and breath, you will probably have generated a great deal of chi. Through conscious imaging, you can use this life force energy to help improve your physical being.

A Few Guidelines

The general sequence you will want to follow is to quietly and slowly awaken your body and your spirit. A few Complete Breaths are important to start your session, then do some slow stretching before you begin one of the vigorous movement systems.

After you have finished the active portion of the session, you need to stabilize the energy you have generated. Passive meditation helps settle the energy. At this point, some students find they have relaxed and centered themselves sufficiently to get closer to true meditation. For this reason, try to give yourself enough passive meditation time to experience this opportunity for real serenity.

Doing a session only once a week is better than not doing it at all, but the best results will be obtained if you can work at least every other day. Try to make some kind of commitment to regular sessions, so that after a few months you will begin to see and feel results. The more you work, the sooner you will achieve change, but you must have patience. We hope you will also practice without haste, not wearily, and not as if it were a great labor.

Don't go beyond the capabilities of your body. If you are unsure, check with a physician about the effect any exercise might have. If an exercise hurts, modify it or save it for another day.

Therapy for the Spirit

You should try to group your exercises according to your reaction to them. Remember what is especially energizing and what cools you down the best. If you become familiar with them all, you will have a good beginning repertoire of tools for special situations.

Here are some suggestions from our experience, to help solve some common complaints:

Keyed up: Yoga, T'ai Chi Ruler, Veil Dancing to very slow music

Sluggish: Red Dragon Chi Kung, T'ai Chi Chi Kung, Earth Dancing

Depressed: Complete Breath, Earth Dancing, Womb Meditation, Bringing Up the Light, or the Anahata Yantra

Flagging libido: Chakra Energizers, Earth Dancing

Fragmented, looking for balance: Nadi Soghana, T'ai Chi Ruler, Dance of the Four Directions

The speed of execution has a lot to do with how each technique affects you. The pace of the complete exhalation and inhalation cycle is the structure, but if you rush the cycle a bit, you may become more energized; if you slow it, you may become more relaxed. Within each technique or system, there is room for individual interpretation for different results. To become familiar with the possibilities, become comfortable with the technique until you are no longer doing it, you *are* it. Practice is the only way we know of to achieve this familiarity; there is no substitute for hard work to achieve your goals.

Spiritual Growth and Rejuvenation

Many positive results are possible from the combination of movement and breath. It creates an alchemy with benefits greater than the sum of the parts.

We offer this information to a wide audience. Readers may come with some spiritual background, and some will have no experience at all but are seeking information. For this reason, we do not go into great detail on many of the areas, leaving it to the reader to research his or her own particular needs.

Many Eastern philosophies are now accessible and better understood than in the past. Some of you may be intrigued with the possibility of spiritual enlightenment, which has drawn increasing interest in America in recent years. Some of you may even come seeking physical immortality. Others will simply want to learn to live in the moment.

Some readers may come for the solace of a philosophy similar to popular Western religions which explains away their mistakes and problems without placing responsibility on the individual. In this case, it will be nearly impossible for that person to find what he or she seeks within this book.

Since there are several important benefits of movement and breath exercises, such as physical toning, weight control, and mental clarity, your main goal could be any one or all of these. Almost everyone today is somewhat familiar with the Oriental approach to exercise and relaxation of mind and body. Yoga and T'ai Chi in many forms have been introduced throughout America in the last few decades. There are already many versions offerred, according to the styles of different teachers and philosophies, but most varieties are similar.

Among our readers, perhaps there will be several whose goal is rejuvenation. For these seekers, no spiritual development is sought in itself, but a return to youthful vigor of mind and body.

This is not a goal to be ashamed of. In fact, for some it may be the most compelling reason of all, the one that actually keeps them working regularly. This is a goal to which almost everyone can relate.

It may be difficult to concentrate solely upon your physical bones and body and increased brain clarity. Always remember, once you begin the adventure you will find many things changing in all facets of your being, whether you truly wish it or not.

How Physical Exercise Rejuvenates

Have you noticed that when you have a cold, you feel the worst when you stop to rest? Activity seems to obscure our symptoms. In fact, working up a sweat flushes out our system, making us feel better, no matter how good or bad we felt before we started.

Conventional medicine is learning that some of these results are tied to the release of natural pain relievers known as endorphins and enkephalins. These chemicals are able to change our perception of pain, but the facts on how it happens aren't fully known yet. In fact, the whole stream of chemical secretions produced by the body, known as hormones, forms an intricate web of life of which science knows very little.

We believe that to break out of the traditional aging pattern, you need, depending on your age and state of health, to either return to or continue the level of hormone production that your body supported at the peak of youth and vitality. In some cases, if you never had a fully functioning internal system, you will want to improve on your baseline. You want your hormone production to be the best it can be. This return to proper hormonal function will begin to occur with the balancing effects of movement and breath exercises.

Hormones and the Flow of Chi

Hormones, though not completely understood, have a powerful influence on health and well-being. These minute secretions are produced all along the central body meridian by internal organs and glands which are a part of the body's endocrine system. These hormonal secretions are complex chemicals released directly into the

Seventy-five years young,
She dances in beauty —
Her feet light
Her heart full of joy.

bloodstream. Most physiological processes of the body are known to be controlled by them. So, though you may have always understood that physical activity helps the body keep itself in shape by keeping muscles firm and bones strong, you may not have realized how important hormonal functioning is in the overall health of the body. It is known that hormones are usually produced in response to signals by the nervous system and the sensory organs. Also, the chemical messages in hormones released by one part of the body trigger a particular release of hormones at another site.

You'll recognize the names of some of the more familiar hormones: cortisone, epinephrine (adrenaline), histamine, hydrocortisone, insulin, melatonin, progesterone, and testosterone. Endorphins and enkephalins are less familiar, and many questions remain as to why and where they are produced. Some of their forms are considered to be hormones; some are not. Their influence as analgesics (which simply means they relieve pain without causing loss of consciousness) is being studied. They also seem to act as antidepressants. Their calming and moderating influence on the pituitary gland and its production of hormones is fascinating, to say the least.

Hormones help control automatic processes such as breathing, heart rate, and the digestive system. They regulate body temperature, sleep, hunger, thirst, urination, sexual drive, and other emotions. And you thought *you* were in control! You really are in control, of course, especially if you can improve the health of the glands and organs of your endocrine system through your choice of activities.

All of this information about how our body functions merely underlines our inescapable conclusion: for your body to function properly and for the aging process to be slowed, you need regular physical exercise.

When disorders of your endocrine system occur and hormone production, assimilation, and communication do not operate perfectly, you can not only age more quickly, you can develop serious physical problems. Some problems that are known to have been brought on at least in part by failures in the hormonal system are obesity, listlessness, weight loss, acne, nervousness, mumps, ulcers, abnormal height, mental retardation, diabetes, immune deficiencies, too low or too high blood pressure, panic attacks, and depression — just to name a few.

For thousands of years, many cultures, especially the Chinese, have placed great emphasis on treating the energy body. Without empirical experimentation, or research and development as we know it today, they studied how to treat bodies which were out of balance, with blockages in the systems of energy circulation. They treated the energy body itself, returning body processes to a vigorous and healthy state. We know now that this flow of energy, called chi, is tied closely to the endocrine system. The traditional systems of movement and breath provided an internal massage to glands and organs. Systems became unblocked. Internal breath training and creative visualization increased the flow of energy that careful physical exercise had begun. The end product of the strong spirit, or shen, often resulted in an increased life span.

Illness is directly related to the flow of energy in the physical and spiritual body. Therefore, developing the flow of this energy will help you heal yourself.

Anahata, the Heart Chakra

In the past, there has been a tendency to overlook or bypass Anahata in spiritual development. When Anahata is not emphasized, undesirable and dark spiritual growth can result.

In both Eastern and Western cultures, the spirit of the heart is often seen as a weakness, when it can actually make you so strong that you are impervious to all outside influences, accepting life as it is. Requiring no conditions, with no anxieties for the future nor guilt from the past, nor awareness of the egotistical "I," an open Anahata will lead you to want what you have and not what you can't have.

Consider Mercury, the nearest planet to Earth. It orbits around the sun, accomplishing its own revolutions, existing on its own terms. We know Mercury exists because we have read and been told about it. Some of us attach significance to it astrologically. But what is actually occurring at this moment on Mercury is really of no consequence to us in our daily lives and it in no way sidetracks us in any way from what is important to us. In other words, we accept Mercury unconditionally.

In the same manner, a balanced Anahata takes note of egotistical thoughts, judgments of others, and similar mental garbage. It lets these thoughts within itself and in others pass by, never attaching enough importance to get involved, never being in a position of needing to judge someone or even of needing to forgive someone.

As you allow your Anahata to flower, we believe that you must get used to sidestepping the cultural environment which tries to teach that the heart is too vulnerable to be open.

Challenge of the Aquarian Age: An Open Heart

In most of us, the first three chakras are well developed, because the human race has existed with these three for ages. The fourth chakra, Anahata, is believed by many to be the next stage of spiritual development in this coming New Age. As the Aquarian Age dawns, unknown and frightening territory is being consciously opened and explored by many for the first time.

The hearts of most of us open occasionally — but almost always shut again immediately, because the heart can be most frightening if you aren't often in that space. It is a "cliffhanger" place to be. The heart area feels weak because it is like a sponge absorbing input of the sort we usually armor ourselves against.

Your Anahata itself is unconditional, but all its input will be filtered through the viewpoints of the lower three chakras. Your open heart will probably feel threatened, and will almost always release its precious energy downward into the lower three chakras. In our experience, it will "slam" its own door tightly shut because of this vulnerability.

For example, if someone ignores or shuns you rudely, your Manipura, the power chakra, leaps quickly to your defense: "How dare this person act so to me?" You might proceed through several stages of indignant rage. But to the heart that is secure in itself, such an episode doesn't matter, and you would have no reaction, no rage, because it would not be worth wasting energy on. Do not mistake this as some kind of self-righteous viewpoint; the rebuff really does not matter. There is unlimited strength in unconditional acceptance. It does feel like a somewhat vulnerable and weak position at first, because you are used to viewing life from the level of the lower chakras.

A Yantra for Anahata

We believe that the New Age will be a time when humankind will achieve a greater capacity to enter into the space of the heart. Therefore, we are sharing a yantra for Anahata, as a meditational device.

In the Tantric tradition of India, the heart chakra is symbolized by a six-pointed star. The star is composed of two equilateral triangles. One upward-pointing turquoise blue triangle symbolizes the male or positive energy. One downward-pointing coral red triangle symbolizes female or negative energy.

The golden point in the center is Bindu — that spark of union between yourself and the cosmos. The twelve petals of the lotus are rose pink. The two circles are golden. The frame around the yantra is called Bhupur and is also golden. This sacred design symbolizes unconditional balanced polarity.

To meditate, place your yantra at eye level, perhaps with a candle at either side as the main illumination of the area. Gaze with soft, unfocused eyes at the point of Bindu, trying not to blink too often. As you gaze at the yantra, maintain Moola bandha to help contain your energy. Chant the word "Yam" (*yamm*) to yourself, or the word "Anahata." This will help magnify the energy. As you breathe in, visualize the energy from the star entering your heart area. Feel a warm golden light swelling in your chest, like a flower opening in the sun. It may help you to keep your left hand on your heart area. Tapping this area helps to activate the thymus, the

Anahata Yantra

endocrine gland associated with Anahata. Some scientific research asserts that this gland is highly susceptible to autosuggestion, that saying to yourself, "Life isn't worth living and I wish I could die," can cause your thymus to shrivel up in reaction. Conversely, a positive affirmation, "Life is beautiful; there is so much for me to live for," can enlarge and strengthen the thymus.

Anytime a certain input creates a downward surge in your energy level, you will feel it as a heaviness in your power chakra. Your names for these sensations may be anger, fear, or frustration. In any case, energy is being pulled down from your heart, and you can choose to consciously draw that energy back into your heart, transforming the unpleasant input into the heart space where it can be lost into unconditional acceptance.

Drawing Your Own Heart Yantra

There is great magical power in creating your own yantra. You don't need artistic talent or expensive materials; what is most important in the process is the part of yourself which goes into your yantra.

You may copy our example, using colored pencils, pastels, or paint. If you wish to be traditional, invest in a small portion of gilt paint for the areas of gold. As you work to create your own sacred design, be sure that your surroundings, your environment, are that of uncluttered serenity. As you work, chant the traditional mantra for the heart chakra, "Yam." If you wish to pursue creating your own yantras, you should acquire *Tools For Tantra*, by Harish Johari, Destiny Books, Vermont, 1986.

As Always, You Have the Choice

We believe that you can live lifetimes on the lower levels of spiritual development, the lower three chakras. The history of humanity thus far proves this. The reason we place such emphasis on the heart is simple. In this time of rapid spiritual advancement of both knowledge and experience, it is possible to become highly developed in the spiritual realms without an open heart. Such a person has chosen the "dark side." We believe an open heart is necessary to one who wishes to choose the "light," and ultimately to attain enlightenment.

The farther you progress into your upper chakra centers, the closer you come to Bindu, that point where we enter cosmic space. Tradition teaches that the more spiritual you become, the less materialistic and grasping your attitudes will become. It is worth mentioning again, too, that this does not mean that the lower chakras are bad. Each level needs to be healthy and strong as you progress upward through the centers of your being. A tree needs strong roots to reach for the sky. If your lower chakras are not strong, entering your heart space could prove difficult, frightening, and probably impossible to maintain.

Rebirthing Can Open Your Heart

All the words in all the world's languages put together cannot explain heart space to someone who has not consciously experienced a heart opening, and maintained that opening long enough to decide that there is where they want to be. There are many techniques for opening the heart. One of the best ways, in our opinion, is through techniques such as Tibetan rebirthing and pulsation, and Yogi Nidra. Rebirthing techniques are powerful tools, so make your selection of a practitioner carefully.

Meeting Life in the Middle

While on the physical plane, true spirituality is not just beauty, or love, or serenity. Life is held together by opposites. What is on the other side of the coin, the hate, the chaos, the ugliness, is what defines the coin. The coin cannot exist without both sides; an open heart cannot exist without unconditional acceptance from both of its sides, from the lower chakras and from the higher chakras.

Humankind's conditions of life, our "wrongs" and "rights," can be thought of as if they were on a scale. The center of that scale is zero, and is the state of unconditionality. If that center, that zero point, is open, you can go there and be reminded that there really are no conditions at all (except what we inflict upon ourselves). It will be easier for you to remember how important it is to be able to keep that center aware.

That center is total unconditional awareness; the heart space is your threshold to cosmic awareness.

Do not set limits
On your inner universe.
Just as the outer universe
Has no apparent limits
Beyond the farthest
Known star,
Dare to take a
Quantum leap in consciousness.
Go beyond your
Farthest inner star
And discover infinity within.

INDEX

Chakra & Kundalini WORKBOOK

—Dr. Jonn Mumford

For Physical and Spiritual Rejuvenation

The end of a millennium and the close of a century are always marked by tremendous social upheavals and radical political changes. Dr. Swami Gitananda stated in the 1950s that "it used to be the problems of man, now it is man, the problem!"

Chakra & Kundalini Workbook gives you remarkable psycho-physiological techniques to overcome the social and psychological chaos, inherent in the transition. It helps you build a solid experience of inner relaxation that will lead towards better health, a longer life and a greater control over your personal destiny.

The book is unique because it captures the best of the East and the West in a modern synthesis of purely efficient, concise and powerful "psychic" techniques combined with breath and posture.

The book:

❖ Provides a step-by-step guidance to the progressive Mind-Body exercises.

❖ Promotes better health and greater control over your personal destiny.

❖ Helps you in the attainment of an enriched Inner Life and Ultimate Enlightenment.

Demy Size • Pages: 264
Price: Rs. 110/- • Postage: Rs. 15/-

Astrology for Layman

—*Dr. T.M. Rao*

The most comprehensible book to learn Astrology

Astrology today is universally recognised to be a 'science', based on sound mathematical principles and calculations. But while it is easy to agree with this promise, it is difficult to find a well-researched comprehensible book to guide the general reader. Answering this need, 'Astrology for Layman' is designed to bring home to the reader the fundamentals of the discipline along with the predictive aspect. One who reads this book will not only be able to make fairly correct predictions, but will also be encouraged to take to the study of more advanced works.

The book is a complete astrological guide that begins from the basic fundamentals viz. how 12 *rashis* have been formulated, the basic principles of casting a horoscope, what are the qualities ascribed to people born under different signs (for instance, people born under Aries are of independent view), what's the meaning of *Bhavas* (viz. what does a planet indicate in a specific house), what do the *Mahadashas* of different planets mean, what are *'yogas'* (for instance, *'Sakaka yoga'* makes a person stubborn and hated by relatives and *'Parvata yoga'*, makes a person passionate) – besides offering special section on the subjects of matrimony, compatibility along with case studies predicting major events of a person's life like career-change, gain or loss of fortune, etc.

Demy Size • Pages: 184
Price: Rs. 80/- • Postage: Rs. 15/-

Horoscope Reading
Made Easy & Self-Learning

—U.C. Mahajan

*Peep into your and your near
& dear one's future*

Astrology by now is a tried and tested science, backed by centuries of analysis and interpretation. The planetary position in the individual charts, the causes and effects of specific conjunctions, the role of sun signs and ascendants—all the aspects of this discipline have been studied in depth by astrologers.

But for the reader, what makes the difference is the presentation of the material—and that's where this book scores over many others.

With a unique format by making extensive use of tables, point-by-point elucidation, explanatory notes and analysis, the book makes an interesting, easy and lucid readable volume. Backed by a thorough research of ancient astrology books of Urdu and English, the volume is a ready-reckoner for self-learners. What are the remedies for adverse star positions? What makes for long or short lines? How is marital bliss indicated in a particular chart? All this and whatever you're looking for is explained here in depth and detail. A must for every serious student of astrology.

Big Size • Pages: 248
Price: Rs. 150/- • Postage: Rs. 15/-

Vaastu Corrections Without Demolitions

—A.R. Hari

Ensure health, happiness and harmony in your home

This book deals with the problem of correcting defective vaastu field where conventional correction methods cannot be applied. This aspect mainly applies to those who live in rented buildings or apartments.

There can also be cases, where the strength of the building and the cost factor may not allow the use of conventional correction methods. **Vaastu Corrections without Demolitions** helps you to correct Vaastu defects with the help of:

❖ Feng Shui gadgets

❖ Installation of Pyramids, Crystals and Ionisers etc.

Demy Size • Pages: 92
Price: Rs. 96/- • Postage: Rs. 15/-

PRACTICAL HYPNOTISM

—*Dr. Narayan Dutt Shrimali*

Towards the Quest of Awareness

In India, the art and science of hypnotism has been a priceless asset. It has been sanctified by timeless traditions. It was largely from India that the rest of the world learnt, followed and imbibed this knowledge.

Our ancient seers tried to discover the potential powers that lay embedded in the human body. They submitted themselves to the Almighty and went deep into the profound mysteries of the inner self.

On the other hand, the west was merely interested in exhibiting its deeds. It was more interested in showing off its superiority. The western idea, unmistakably was that man is what he himself wills to be. It also felt that man owes nothing whatsoever to the powers beyond, to the Creator and to the power of the soul.

Practical Hypnotism is a study, complete in all respects, which seeks to explain the science of hypnotism in simple, straight forward and unambiguous language. It makes an integrated study of the loftiest thoughts of the western thinkers and yet it heavily draws upon the priceless contemplations of the Indian seers of yore. For having achieved a fine blending of the two powerful strains of scholarship, the volume will commend itself to all strata of readership.

Demy Size • Pages: 236
Price: Rs. 96/- • Postage: Rs. 15/-

Instant Handwriting Analysis

—Ruth Gardner

Do your 'Gs' divulge a sensitive nature? Does your writing slant show you to be impulsive? Find out with Ruth Gardner's **Instant Handwriting Analysis.**

Handwriting patterns signal elements of your unconscious, and reveal your desires, fears, weaknesses, strengths, attitudes and more! With this book, someone who doesn't even know you could learn all about you in just a few moments!

This work covers some of the most important and basic factors of handwriting analysis for the explorer of Graphology — a scientific study on the field.

Now you can analyse your own handwriting and that of friends and family with this easy-to-use book. In just a few moments, you will know what the slant, stroke, word-spacing, margins, size and pressure, letter formations and signature reveal about your personality. You can even learn to change certain aspects of yourself by changing the way you write!

Compare your writing with the samples in this book — it's that simple! There is even a section on doodles. You may find that graphology is your next career or hobby!

Demy Size • Pages: 152
Price: Rs. 96/- • Postage: Rs. 15/-

Taoist Yoga for Better Sex Life

—Eric Steven Yudelove

The Tao is a Chinese expression that literally means 'the way', or in other words, the 'source' of all created beings—living and non-living. And in Taoist yoga, the way is shown to attain heightened physical, mental and sexual energy through Internal Alchemy—which means gathering the energies from the five major internal organs—heart, lungs, kidneys, liver and spleen, harmonizing it and changing from the negative to positive.

This channelization of the energy in the body produces renewed sexual utility and a rejuvenated mind and spirit. The process includes a system of simple breathing and other exercises that anybody can do. Through Abdominal Breathing, Reverse Breathing, Testicle and Ovarian Breathing, the book goes on to describe Sexual Kung Fu, Hair Breathing, Standing Chi Kung, Rooting Practice, fusion of five elements, Breathing into hips, ankles and knees to connecting the sensual organs and sexual energy massage.

Big Size • Pages: 195
Price: Rs. 175/- • Postage: Rs. 20/-
